One Hundred Strength Exercises

One Hundred Strength Exercises

Ed McNeely

ILLUSTRATIONS BY MARTY BEE

Bb BURFORD BOOKS

Printed in the United States of America.

10 9 8 7 6 5 4 3 2

Library of Congress Cataloging-in-Publication Data

McNeely, Ed (Edward), 1967-
 One hundred strength routines / by Ed McNeely.
    p. cm.
 ISBN 1-58080-132-3 (pbk.)
 1. Weight lifting. 2. Muscle strength. I. Title.

 GV546.3.M35 2005
 613.7'13—dc22

                          2005001764

Contents

Introduction

Most of us are familiar with the benefits of strength training for athletic performance: increased strength and power, improved speed, greater muscle mass and a reduction in the rate of injuries. While all these adaptations are important for sports, they are also valuable for the non-athlete.

Prevent Injuries

Whether you are playing a sport or walking on an icy street, injuries can occur at any time. Stronger bones, muscles, joints, and connective tissue will make you more resistant to the injuries that occur during falls or collisions with an opponent, but the everyday benefits of strength training come in the prevention of the chronic shoulder, knee, and back pains that can make daily life more difficult.

Muscle imbalances, either bilateral differences between the right and left sides of the body, or agonist/antagonist imbalances in muscles that are on opposite sides of a joint, have been implicated in the development of injury. Muscle imbalances cause the body to move incorrectly, resulting in excessive strain on some muscles and joints. Some studies have noted that a muscle imbalance of greater than 10% between the right and left sides of the body increase the risk of injury by 20 times.

Most sports, and many of our daily activities force us into a position where one side of the body is used more than the other, leading to muscle imbalances. Strength training the right and left sides separately, using dumbbells and unilateral machines, can correct many of these imbalances and decrease your risk of developing chronic injuries and aches.

The Anti-Aging Formula

There is a relationship between muscle size and strength. This does not mean that you need to develop huge muscles to become strong, because even small increases in muscle size will dramatically increase strength. There is a decline in muscle mass and strength as we age, leading to chronic aches and pains, difficulty performing daily activities, and a loss of independence and quality of life. This deterioration in performance can start as early as age 30 and gets worse every year, but don't despair. A moderately intense full-body strength training program, performed two or three times per week, can delay and even reverse the loss of muscle mass.

It's never too late to start a strength training program. Muscle mass and strength can increase in people well into their 70s. There are many retired people who, after taking up strength training, are physically stronger and more fit than they were in their youth.

Strength training is a life-long physical activity that, in addition to the performance benefits already discussed, carries with it a variety of health benefits, including improved blood lipid profiles and increased bone density.

ALTERED BLOOD LIPID PROFILES

High blood cholesterol levels have been associated consistently with the development of heart disease. Controlling cholesterol levels—increasing HDL, the good cholesterol or decreasing LDL, the bad cholesterol—can lessen the incidence of heart disease. Strength training has been consistently shown to decrease total cholesterol and improve the LDL/HDL ratio that is strongly linked to health problems by decreasing LDL and increasing HDL levels.

INCREASED BONE DENSITY

Osteoporosis is a problem in modern society, particularly for seniors. After age 35 bone density starts to decline at a rate of 1 to 3% per year. While this may not sound like much, the cumulative effect of years of bone loss can result in fractures and frailty in old age. We have known for more than a century that there is a relationship between mechanical loading of bone and bone density and strength. Certain types and volumes of physical activity increase bone mineral density (BMD), while immobilization, lack of weight-bearing activity and prolonged bed rest decrease bone density. Strength training, taken up after age 35, is one of the best ways to slow or halt the normal loss of bone density. Taking strength training up earlier in life may provide even more benefit. Strength training during your teens and early 20s can increase bone density, providing you with a buffer against future bone loss so that even if there is a period in your life when you are unable to exercise to maintain your bone density you have some to spare.

Strength Training for Children

The use of strength training for children has gained acceptance as part of a well-rounded fitness program. The risks of injury to children during strength training are lower than those of most other popular participation sports, and the notion that resistance training will damage growth plates in the bones has not been borne out by research. A well designed strength program that focuses on the individual physical and psychological maturity level of the child can not only decrease the risk of injury in other sports, but it can also improve bone density, positively alter body composition, and increase the child's self esteem. An early, positive strength-training experience can become a life long appreciation for physical activity.

Based on the position statement of the National Strength and Conditioning Association, and reviews by the American Academy of Pediatrics, the following guidelines for developing strength training programs for prepubescent children are recommended:

➤ Young athletes require a medical examination prior to strength training, including assessing their physical maturity level.

➤ There is no lower limit on age when a child can start strength training. Decisions on starting age should be based more on the child's emotional maturity and ability to follow directions than on physical development.

➤ Provide adequate supervision and instruction. The athlete-coach ratio should not exceed 10:1 with a ratio of 5:1 preferred. This should help the athlete learn proper technique. Most strength-training injuries occur because of poor exercise technique.

➤ Prohibit maximal lifts. This helps prevent possible injury to the bones' growth zones. Since children and young teenagers are often competitive and want to see how much they can lift, it may be necessary to limit prepubertal athletes to body weight exercises (push ups, sit ups, pull ups, etc.).

➤ Ensure that the athlete has the emotional maturity to accept and follow directions. Athletes risk injuring themselves and others when strength training if they cannot follow directions and safety guidelines.

➤ Consider the unique physical and psychological makeup of each athlete. Since the rate of emotional and physical maturity varies from person to person, an individualized training program will help improve performance and decrease the chance of injury.

➤ Include strength training in a conditioning program. Expose young athletes to a variety of activities and movement patterns. Limiting training to a specific activity can slow the athlete's overall development.

➤ Keep training fun for the young athlete. This can help develop a lifelong appreciation for fitness and sport. The length of the athlete's career can be increased if the level of enjoyment is high.

➤ Develop or adopt a set of weight training rules and regulations.

Starting children into a strength training program at an early age may help them develop the skills and attitudes needed to make strength training part of a lifelong commitment to exercise. By establishing a written set of rules and guidelines based on sound scientific evidence, coaches and physical educators can safely and effectively make strength training a part of youth sport and fitness programs. Adequate supervision will ensure that the risks of injury often attributed to strength training are minimized while the benefits, which include increased strength, improved blood lipid profile, enhanced motor skills, and decreased rate of injury in other sports, are maximized in an enjoyable setting.

Safe and Effective Training

Strength training is one of the safest forms of physical activity, having a much lower injury rate than other common recreational activities like basketball, tennis, golf, or running. As long as some simple guidelines are followed, your strength training experience can be injury free.

TECHNIQUE FIRST

Approximately 80 percent of the injuries that occur during strength training happen because of poor technique. The purpose of this book is to help you learn how to safely and properly perform a variety of exercises, but ultimately you have the responsibility of ensuring that you are doing the exercises properly. If you are not sure how to do an exercise after reading the descriptions it may be worth investing a few dollars to have a personal trainer or strength coach spend an hour showing you the exercises that are causing confusion.

A major cause of technical errors is training to failure, meaning training to the point that you cannot go further. When you push yourself to the point that you can no longer lift the weight, the last couple of repetitions are usually done with imperfect technique. During the first 4 to 6 months of training, when your body is still learning to perfect the movements, avoid training to failure. Instead stop the set when you or your training partner first notices that your technique is starting to break down.

NO PAIN NO GAIN

One of the most persistent myths in strength training is that muscle soreness represents progress and that if you are not sore the next day you did not work hard enough. This is based on the notion that breaking down the muscles causes them to increase in size and strength. This is an overly simplistic approach to a series of very complex physiological changes at the cellular level, involving hormones, growth factors, and nutrients. There is little scientific evidence that breaking down muscle is the best stimulus for adaptation.

While it is common to be sore for a few days when you take up a training program for the first time, attempting to be sore after every training session will quickly lead to overtraining and a variety of injuries, particularly tendonitis, because the tendons do not recover as quickly from the stress of training as do the muscles.

PROGRESSION

It is important to challenge yourself during a training session. The overload principle, one of the primary principles of training, states that the muscles must be put under a continually greater stress if they are to continue to adapt. On the other hand, the need for progress must be tempered with adequate recovery so that your body can adapt to the stress. It is human nature to jump in to a new activity with enthusiasm, and while you may have the time to work out six days per week it does not mean you should. When starting a strength training program begin with two sessions per week, increase to three after 3 to 4 months, and then move onto a more advanced program, training four or more times per week after 6 to 8 months of training.

REST

Strength training affects more than the muscles—bones, connective tissue, your heart, and nervous system are all stressed during training as well. These organs and tissues do not all recover or adapt at the same rate, so while the muscles might have recovered from a training session, your connective tissue may still need more time. Since it is not possible to measure recovery in multiple systems it is essential to plan a recovery week into your training. A recovery week occurs every four to six weeks and is a week where you decrease the frequency and intensity of your training sessions by cutting the number of exercises and the weight you use in half. This gives all the tissues and organs a break, allowing them to recover and improve at a faster rate.

VARIETY

Your body adapts to an exercise very quickly. One of the reasons that there are 100 exercises in this book is to allow you to change them frequently. Varying the exercises will help you progress faster and prevent overuse injuries that may occur when the same exercise is done for too long. Exercises should be changed every 3 to 4 weeks.

These guidelines will increase the effectiveness of your program and help keep you injury free, but common sense is your strongest ally. If something does not feel right during training, don't do it. If you are feeling too tired for a training session take an extra day off; unless you are training for a major sporting competition an extra day off is not going to affect your training.

CHAPTER 1

The Basics

The popularity of strength training has increased immensely over the past twenty-five years, moving from a fringe activity practiced only by bodybuilders and competitive lifters to become a mainstream activity that is recognized not only for its performance-enhancing benefits, but also for its ability to improve health and quality of life.

A well designed strength-training program offers a wealth of health and performance improvements, from increasing strength and power to improving bone density, altering cholesterol and triglyceride levels, and changing body shape and composition.

Before you begin your strength program, or start reading through the exercise descriptions contained in this book, it is essential that you are familiar with some basic concepts in strength training.

Muscle Actions

A muscle action refers to the state of activity of a muscle. Muscles are capable of three types of activity:

➤ *Concentric* muscle actions involve the shortening of the muscle and usually occur when the body or a weight is lifted.

➤ *Eccentric* muscle actions involve lengthening of a muscle and are usually seen when a weight is being lowered or the body is decelerated. Landing from a jump involves an eccentric contraction of the quadriceps muscles.

➤ *Isometric* muscle actions involve no change in the length of a muscle. The maintenance of body positions during strength training exercises is accomplished through isometric muscle actions.

Training Variables
SETS AND REPETITIONS

In strength training a movement cycle consists of a concentric and an eccentric contraction. This cycle is known as a repetition or "rep." When several repetitions are performed in a row, this is known as a set. The number of sets and repetitions that are performed during a training session depends upon the age and experience of the athlete as well as the goals of the training session.

This information is covered in more detail through out the rest of this book.

INTENSITY

Intensity is the tension or stress put on the muscle. Intensity is influenced by the number of sets and reps and the rest between sets, but intensity is mainly affected by the amount of weight that is being lifted. Intensity is relative: what is intense for one person may be easy for another.

VOLUME

Volume is the total amount of work the muscles do in an exercise or session. It is most often determined by multiplying the sets and reps for each exercise to get a total number of repetitions per exercise. In some cases this is multiplied by the amount of weight lifted for each exercise to get a total amount of weight lifted in the workout.

REST

Rest refers to the amount of time that is taken between sets or exercises. For instance, if you do a set of bench press exercises and then wait three minutes before you do another set, your rest period was three minutes.

RECOVERY

Recovery refers to the time between training sessions for the same muscle group or exercise. If you did bench press as part of your workout on Monday, and then did it again on Wednesday, you would have had two days, or 48 hours, recovery.

Body Planes and Motion

Knowing how the body moves is an important first step when taking up strength training. There are three planes of movement, corresponding to the three dimensions of space, and four major types of movement.

SAGITTAL PLANE

The sagittal plane is a vertical plane, passing from front to back, dividing the body into right and left halves.

FRONTAL PLANE

The frontal plane is a vertical plane dissecting the body from one side to the other, dividing it into front (anterior) and back (posterior) halves.

TRANSVERSE PLANE

The transverse plane is a horizontal plane dividing the body into upper and lower halves.

FLEXION

Flexion is a type of movement where the angle at a joint diminishes. For instance, there is flexion of the elbow occurring in the arm curl exercise.

EXTENSION

Extension is the opposite of flexion, a movement where the angle at the joint increases. The straightening of the arm as the weight is returned to the starting position in the arm curl is an example of elbow extension.

ABDUCTION

Abduction occurs when a limb is moved away from the midline of the body. This term is most often used in sideward movements of the upper limb away from the body, as in the lateral raise.

ADDUCTION

Adduction occurs when a limb moves towards the midline of the body. This is the opposite of abduction.

Anatomy

In order to design your training program and fully understand which exercises to choose you need a basic understanding of the anatomy of the major muscles. The figures on pages 22 and 23 highlight the major muscles of the front and back of the body.

Major Muscle Groups

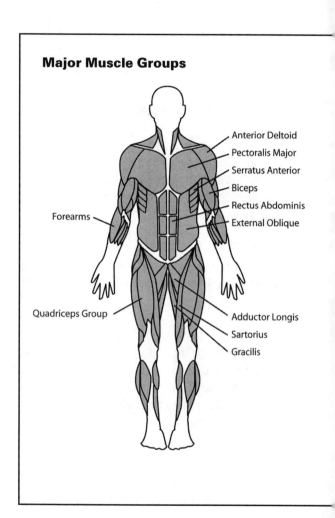

Anterior Deltoid

Pectoralis Major

Serratus Anterior

Biceps

Rectus Abdominis

External Oblique

Forearms

Quadriceps Group

Adductor Longis

Sartorius

Gracilis

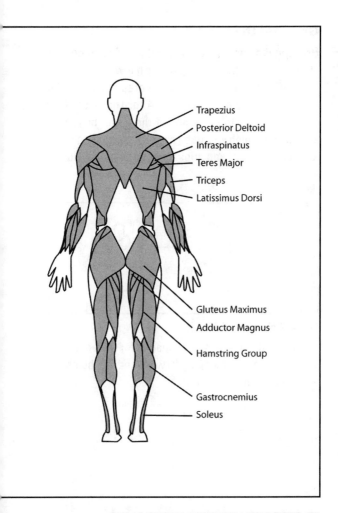

Trapezius
Posterior Deltoid
Infraspinatus
Teres Major
Triceps
Latissimus Dorsi

Gluteus Maximus
Adductor Magnus

Hamstring Group

Gastrocnemius
Soleus

...ping the bar

Gripping the bar is an often-overlooked component of strength training. A firm grip on the bar will increase the amount of weight you can lift by creating a solid link between your hands and the bar. A solid grip also allows you to contract the muscles of the upper body more effectively, which will stabilize you during lifting. There are five different hand grips that can be employed:

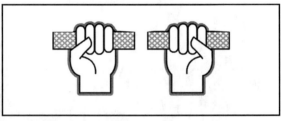

UNDERHAND GRIP

The underhand grip is used mainly for arm-curl exercises. The palms are facing forward and the thumbs are wrapped around the bar.

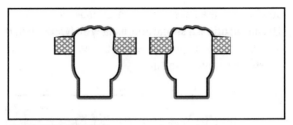

OVERHAND GRIP

This is the most common grip. The palms are placed over the bar and are facing away from the body. This grip is used in pressing movements, squats, pulldowns, various rows, and many tricep exercises.

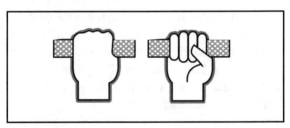

MIXED GRIP

The mixed grip is used during various deadlifts and prevents the bar from moving away from the body. One hand is placed in an overhand grip and the other in an underhand grip position. The choice of which way your hands go is a matter of personal preference. Try both configurations and use the one that is most comfortable. The mixed grip is a strong grip, usually allowing a heavier weight to be used than would be the case with the overhand or underhand grips.

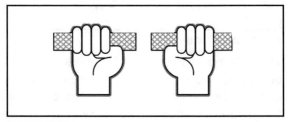

HOOK GRIP

The hook grip is used by Olympic-style weightlifters for cleans and snatches. It is the strongest of the grips. The hands are placed in an overhand position on the bar, the thumbs are then wrapped underneath the other fingers and squeezed tightly. This grip will be quite painful the first couple of times it is used, particularly if you forget to squeeze as hard as possible.

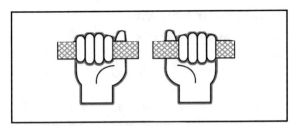

THUMBLESS OR OPEN GRIP

If you read fitness magazines you will undoubtedly see a picture of someone using a thumbless grip, where the bar is placed on the heel of the hand and the fingers, but not the thumb, are wrapped around the bar. This is the least secure of the grips and provides the least control over the bar. It doesn't allow the bar to be squeezed as tightly and compromises the stability of the rest of the body. This grip is generally not recommended as using it invites a greater risk of dropping the bar. Many times people who are bench pressing and have had the bar roll out of their hands, falling on their chest and causing serious injury. This grip should only be used as a last resort if you have wrist or shoulder problems that prevent you from using the other grips, and care should always be exercised when using it.

Weight Room Etiquette

Facility rules and codes of conduct make the weight room safe for all users and supervisors but it is the unwritten rules that make the experience more enjoyable. Many of the rules of etiquette in the weight room are based on common sense and good manners. Pay attention to what you are doing and be aware of those around you. Treat others as you would want to be treated, act in a courteous manner, and these rules will be easy to follow.

➤ Always ask if anyone is using a piece of equipment before moving it or taking the weights off.

➤ If you need a piece of equipment someone else is using ask if you can work in with them. If they say no you will just have to wait; first come, first served.

➤ Do not stand on a platform when someone else is lifting. Not only is this dangerous to you and the lifter, but it is also distracting.

➤ Do not stand directly in someone's line of sight. During lifts like squats, deadlifts, and the weightlifting movements it is important to look straight ahead and keep your eyes focused on a spot in the distance. If you are working near someone who is doing these lifts, try not to stand directly in front of them unless you are at least 10 feet away. If you are closer than this your movement will make it difficult for them to find their focus point and could cause them to use bad technique and injure themselves.

➤ Use only the space you need. Weightlifting platforms and power racks are intended for lifts like squats, deadlifts, weightlifting movements, and other heavy power activities—they are not a place to do arm curls, sit ups, etc. You may have seen some bodybuilder in a magazine placing their bar on a power rack to do arm curls but this behavior will inevitably annoy people who are waiting for the rack. There are lots of other places where you can do your arm curls and other single-joint exercises.

➤ Wear clean clothes. You may be able to wear the same workout gear for a couple of sessions if you don't sweat too much but you need to change everything at least every third workout. You may not notice the smell, but others will.

➤ Stop the screaming. There is absolutely no need to scream and yell during a training session. If you can't get yourself psyched up to do a lift without screaming you should consider picking up a good sports psychology book to help you with this problem. Screaming during the lift doesn't help you either; in fact, yelling at the wrong time can actually cause you to expel the air from your lungs too early, destabilizing your trunk and increasing the risk of injury. This is not to say that you can't make some noise when lifting; as you exhale near the finish of a lift there is bound to be some grunting and noise. But you shouldn't intentionally be yelling and screaming.

➤ Don't offer unsolicited advice. When you are in a gym doing your workout, that is what you are there to do. While there is a social component to strength training, unless you are specifically asked for advice or help, do not walk around the gym sharing your expertise with everyone. While you may find a couple of people who are grateful for your input, you will find just as many who are annoyed by this behavior. In some cases you may offer advice to someone who knows a lot more about training than you do and they will make you look foolish. If you really want to dispense training advice to people, consider it as a career and become a certified personal trainer or strength coach.

➤ Respect the gym community. There are many different types of gyms: fitness centers where people who are interested in improving their health and fitness train, hardcore body building gyms where posing in mirrors and loud music are the norm, and hardcore lifting gyms where serious lifters go to lift very heavy weights. Each gym attracts it's own clientele and has it's own code of behavior. If you are a serious lifter and find yourself in a health and fitness gym, it is up to you to adapt to their standards of conduct, not the other way around. You wouldn't expect to move into a seniors community and have loud wild parties all night long, and you shouldn't expect everyone else to change or accept your behavior if it isn't part of the norm for the gym.

CHAPTER 2

Equipment and Accessories

Whether you are going to be using this book at the local gym or you plan to outfit your basement as a home gym, you have lots of options when it comes to equipment and accessories.

Free Weights

Free weights consist of barbells—long bars with fixed or adjustable weights—and dumbbells, smaller handheld fixed or adjustable weights. Barbells come in two sizes: standard, which has a uniform diameter of about 1 1/8 inches, and Olympic, with the same bar diameter and a 2" diameter outside sleeve where the plates are loaded. Weight plates for either system range from 1.25 lbs to 100 lbs. Olympic plates are also available in kilogram increments.

There are many varieties of dumbbells; fixed dumbbells are the preferred type for institutional use as they are safer than the adjustable dumbbells. The most common types of fixed dumbbells are the hex and plate dumbbells. The hex dumbbells are solid hexagonal shaped pieces of iron held together with a center bar. The center bar is placed in a hole that has been drilled part way through the weight. These are usually much less expensive than the plate loaded dumbbells, which consist of individual weight plates permanently loaded onto a dumbbell handle. Hex dumbbells are excellent for home or low-use facilities like a personal training studio. Larger commercial gyms will typically use plate-loaded dumbbells.

Adjustable dumbbells are frequently used in home gyms. The traditional plate loaded dumbbell takes a lot of time to load and you must make sure that the collars on the ends of the bar are tight so that the plates do not fall off during a set.

Benches and Racks

Fixed and adjustable benches and racks compliment free weights, improving safety and increasing the variety of exercises that can be performed. Benches and racks come in either institutional grade or home gym grade. The weight and size of the steel used in institutional equipment is much higher than in home gym equipment and the welds are usually stronger, making the equipment more durable and safer in high use areas. Pay attention to the maximum load that the equipment is designed to handle. Squat racks and power cages should be able to handle at least 1500 lbs, while benches should be able to hold at least 1000 lbs.

Fixed benches for bench press and incline press are standard in most training facilities, as are flat and adjustable utility benches that can be moved around the room. Adjustable uprights on flat and incline benches are essential in commercial settings so that they can be adjusted to accommodate a variety of arm lengths.

Most benches are 16 to 18 inches high. It is essential that you are able to place your feet flat on the floor when using a bench; this increases stability and safety of the lift. If lower benches are not available, foot blocks made from 2" x 10" boards will need to be made.

Weight Machines

The past twenty years have seen an explosion in the number of weight machine manufacturers around the world. Machines have become very popular in fitness clubs because they are safe and require little instruction. The down side is that they are quite expensive and require regular maintenance and cleaning.

While there are a variety of different types of resistance that machines provide, the majority of machines are plate loaded or stack loaded. Plate-loaded machines use the same weight plates as free weight bars, and may be the best option if you are purchasing free weights in addition to machines. They are often less expensive than the stack loaded machines and have fewer pulleys and cables to replace and maintain. Plate loaded machines allow smaller weight increments to be used than most stack machines and can be loaded heavier than many of the standard weight stacks.

Elastic Resistance

Rubber tubing and giant elastic bands have become more popular in recent years as strength-training accessories. Combining rubber tubing and some broom sticks will allow a budget strapped school to offer an effective and safe introductory strength course with a minimal cash outlay and limited space. Rubber tubing can be purchased through many exercise equipment catalogues like Power Systems, or you can buy surgical tubing from a surgical supply distributor and cut it to any length you desire. With a little creative thinking tubing can be used to simulate almost every free-weight exercise. Lengths of tube can be looped over a broom handle to simulate barbell exercises like squats, deadlifts, and presses; individual lengths of tubing can be used to simulate dumbbell exercises. Storage hooks are all that is needed to keep tubing tangle-free and out of the way when it is not in use.

While tubing-based programs will enable you to learn the basic body positions and movements, there is a limit to the amount of strength that will be gained from tubing and broom handles alone because the amount of resistance that can be attached safely is low compared to either machines or free weights.

Choosing the Right Equipment

If you are working out at a commercial facility you will have access to most types of equipment, forcing you to make a decision between free weights and machines. Unless you are training solely for aesthetic purposes, free weights are generally considered a better training tool than machines. Free weights offer an unlimited number of exercises from one set of weights, while machines (other than cable machines) are single-purpose units with a fixed movement plane and range.

Free weights require the smaller stabilizer muscles to work to balance the barbell or dumbbell, training them so that they are strengthened along with the major muscle groups, which helps to create more functional fitness. Machines, because of their fixed-path, counter weights, do not require the stabilizers to work as much, potentially contributing to muscle imbalances. For these reasons the majority of the exercises in this book use barbells and dumbbells rather than machines.

Personal Equipment and Weight Training Accessories

WEIGHT TRAINING BELTS

Next time you are in the weight room look around and see how many people are wearing belts. You will probably find a lot of people using a belt—but few who actually need one.

The Purpose of Weight Belts

During weight training the forces acting on the spine can exceed 10,000 N (Newtons, the unit of force)—approximately 2200 lbs. Forces this high have the ability to damage the spine seriously. The compressive loads on the spine during exercises such as the squat can be as high as 10 times body weight. In order to prevent injury during lifting, the body increases intra-abdominal pressure, which helps stabilize the lumbar spine during heavy lifting tasks.

When the diaphragm and other abdominal muscles contract, they press against the fluids within the abdomen. The fluids, and tissue that surround them, are pressed against the spine and aid in supporting the spine during lifting. Lifting belts help to increase this intra-abdominal pressure. This means that weight belts have the potential to decrease the compressive forces acting upon the spine during lifting, potentially making it safer.

Proper Use of Lifting Belts

Many people wear a belt for all exercises. This is unnecessary and potentially dangerous. When a belt is worn, the activity of the *erector spinae* (lower back muscles) and the various abdominal muscles is decreased.

If these muscles are not allowed to play a supportive role during strength training, they will not be able to play that role when a situation arises outside the gym, where lifting has to be done and a belt is not available. This could increase the possibility of lower back injury.

If the belt is used properly, the lower back and abdominal muscles can receive adequate stimulation. Belts should not be worn during exercises where the back is not directly stressed. Exercises like bench press, pulldowns, arm curls, chin ups and so on create very little compressive force on the spine. When belts are worn during these exercises it is more of a fashion statement than a protective tool.

The belt should only be worn when the load used exceeds 70 to 80% of the maximum amount of weight that you can lift. Even then, it is not necessary to wear a belt. Competitive weightlifters train and compete with maximal weights without wearing a belt and have very low rates of back injury.

There are two types of belt that are commonly used. (1) The thin belt, which is wide at the back and tapers in the front. (2) The thick belt, common among powerlifters, is four inches wide all the way around. The wider surface provided by the thick belt that your stomach can press against makes it more effective for increasing intra-abdominal pressure and is the belt of choice for most lifting. However, the thin belt may be better for people with very short torsos or those involved in Olympic-style lifts, where a thick belt may catch the lower ribs and cause pain.

A belt can be a useful tool during strength training if used properly. However, overdependence on the belts may increase the risk of injury in non-training situations. As a final thought—competitive powerlifters use a weight belt not only because it acts as an injury-prevention tool, but it also enhances performance. Some lifters report that a belt, when tight enough, can increase the weight they lift by 15 to 35 lbs.

KNEE WRAPS

In many commercial gyms it is common to see people wrapping their knees with a neoprene bandage before squatting. The belief is that the support from the bandage will protect their knees from injury. The truth is that they may be putting their knees at greater risk.

Knee wraps are used by competitive lifters as a performance aid. They are generally not considered an injury-prevention tool. The wraps are wrapped around the leg and knee in a specific pattern and are so tight that the leg cannot be bent until a heavy weight is used in the squat. Some lifters report increasing their squat by as much as 35 lbs as a result of using knee wraps. Most competitive powerlifters will only use the wraps when they get to heavier weights, 85% or more of their maximum, and will only perform 2 to 3 reps per set when wearing knee wraps.

Wrapping the knees for every set and performing lots of reps with wrapped knees can lead to knee injury. The wrap squeezes the kneecap against the other bones of the leg and causes them to rub on the back of the kneecap, causing pain and inflammation. If you like the feeling of warmth knee wraps provide, consider using a loose-fitting knee warmer instead of wraps, which will provide the warmth you seek without compressing your kneecap.

LIFTING STRAPS

Lifting straps are pieces of woven fabric or leather that wrap around your wrist and the bar, essentially tying you to the bar. Lifting straps help you lift weights that you cannot hold onto normally. They are good tools for competitive lifters who are doing partial repetitions with extremely heavy weights. The downside of lifting straps is that over-use of them prevents you from developing good grip strength, creating further reliance on the straps and incomplete strength development.

GLOVES

Gloves are a popular weight-training accessory. They are not a necessary piece of equipment but more of a personal choice. They will prevent the build up of calluses on the hands and can improve grip if your palms get sweaty and you are not allowed to use chalk. If you are involved in a sport where your grip is important you may not want to use gloves. The buildup of calluses on your hands will improve your gripping of other sport implements.

If you do decide to use gloves be sure to purchase gloves that are made for weight training. Bicycle gloves look similar to weight-training gloves but have a padded hand, which is important for shock absorption in cycling, but which will make it more difficult to squeeze and hold onto the bar.

SHOES

There are special shoes available for both weightlifting and powerlifting. Weightlifting shoes have a solid wood, elevated heel that puts your body in a better position for the Olympic-style lifts. They provide good lateral support and are low cut to give foot and ankle mobility. Many power lifters use weightlifting shoes but there are also powerlifting shoes, which are often high cut to help stabilize the ankle, have a flat sole and good lateral support. It is not necessary to use specialized shoes for workouts—any shoe that offers good lateral support is acceptable. Try to avoid running shoes with cushioned heels, as the soft heel makes it more difficult to shift your weight properly from the front to the back of your feet without losing balance.

Belts, gloves, wraps and straps can play a role in training but they are not necessary accessories. Spend some time training without them before deciding to spend money on a piece of equipment you may not really need.

Chest Exercises

CHEST EXERCISES

1 **BENCH PRESS** Lie on your back on a bench press bench with feet spread wide, flat on the floor. Reach up and grasp the bar with an overhand grip, placing your hands just wider than shoulder width apart. Inhale deeply and lift the bar out of the rack to arm's length. Lower the bar under control so that it touches your chest near the base of your sternum; do not bounce the bar off your chest. Press the bar back up to arm's length. Keep your feet planted firmly and your head shoulders and buttocks in contact with the bench throughout the movement. Exhale as you pass through the sticking point near the end of the movement.

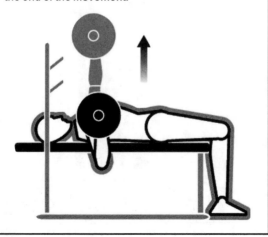

2 INCLINE PRESS Adjust the incline bench press bench so that it is at a 45-degree angle, lie back on the bench with feet spread wide, flat on the floor. Reach up and grasp the bar with an overhand grip, placing your hands just wider than shoulder width apart. Inhale deeply and lift the bar out of the rack to arm's length. Lower the bar under control so that it touches the top part of your chest; do not bounce the bar off your chest. Press the bar back up to arm's length. Keep your feet planted firmly and your head shoulders and buttocks in contact with the bench throughout the movement. Exhale as you pass through the sticking point near the end of the movement.

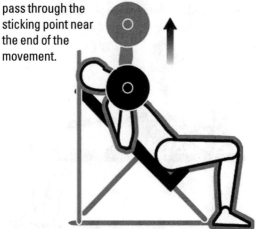

3 DUMBBELL BENCH PRESS Sit on the end of a flat bench with a pair of dumbbells resting on your legs. Lie back on the bench and bring the dumbbells to your chest. Place your feet flat on the floor and turn your hands so the ends of the dumbbells are facing each other. Keeping hands shoulder width apart, press the dumbbells to arm's length. Lower the weight under control until the dumbbells touch the outside of the chest, halfway down your sternum. Keep your feet planted firmly and your head shoulders and buttocks in contact with the bench throughout the movement. When you finish the required number of repetitions place the weights on the floor beside the bench and return to a seated position.

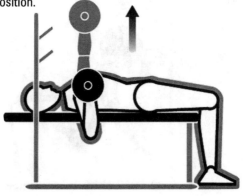

4 DUMBBELL INCLINE PRESS Adjust the incline bench press bench so that it is at a 45-degree angle, lie back on the bench with feet spread wide, flat on the floor. Have a training partner hand you a pair of dumbbells. Turn your hands so the ends of the dumbbells are facing each other. Keeping hands shoulder width apart, press the dumbbells to arm's length. Lower the weight under control until the dumbbells touch the outside of the chest, near the top of your chest. When you are finished have your training partner take the dumbbells from you and place them on the floor.

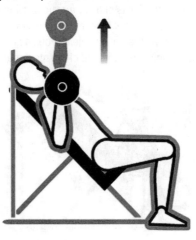

5 DECLINE PRESS Lie on your back on a decline press bench, a bench that is angled down so that your head is lower than your feet, with your feet hooked securely under the leg support. Reach up and grasp the bar with an overhand grip, placing your hands just wider than shoulder width apart. Inhale deeply and lift the bar out of the rack to arm's length. Lower the bar under control so that it touches your chest at the base of your sternum; do not bounce the bar off your chest. Press the bar back up to arm's length. Keep your head shoulders and buttocks in contact with the bench throughout the movement. The range of motion is shorter for the decline press than either the bench or incline press, allowing you to use slightly more weight. Exhale as you pass through the sticking point near the end of the movement.

6 **DUMBBELL FLYS** Sit on the end of a flat bench with a pair of dumbbells seated on your legs. Lie back on the bench and bring the dumbbells to your chest. Place your feet flat on the floor, press the dumbbells to arm's length and turn your hands so your palms are facing each other. Bend your elbows slightly so that they are not locked. Lower the weight to the side until the dumbbells are parallel to the floor. Then pull the weights back up to the starting position, keeping the elbows slightly bent throughout the movement. The movement used in the fly is similar to hugging a tree, with the weight following a semi-circular path.

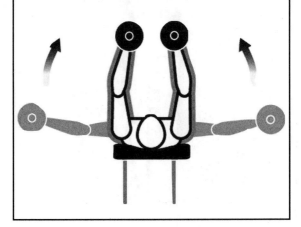

7 CABLE CROSSOVERS Stand between two high pulleys with your feet shoulder-width apart. Grasp the handles with an overhand grip. Incline your trunk to about 30 degrees and, with elbows slightly bent, pull the handles together in front of your body. The movement used in the cable crossover is similar to hugging a tree, with the weight following a semi-circular path.

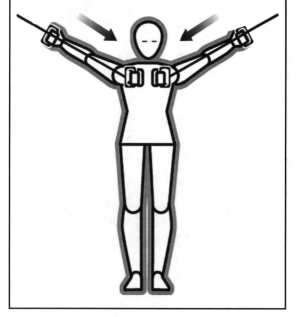

8 DIPS Grasp parallel bars and raise the body up until the arms are fully locked out, knees are bent and feet are crossed. Slowly bend the elbows and lower the body between the bars, until the arms are fully bent and there is a 90-degree angle between your upper arm and forearm. Straighten the elbows and press the body back up until the starting position is reached.

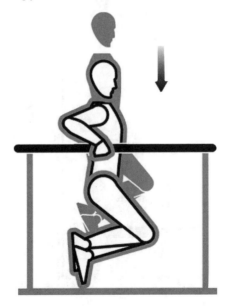

9 SEATED BENCH PRESS Sit on a bench press machine and adjust the seat so that the handles are mid-chest high. Grasp the handles with an overhand grip and press them to arm's length. Return the handles towards the chest, stopping just before the plates on the weight stack touch. Keep your feet flat on the floor and head and shoulders against the machine throughout the movement.

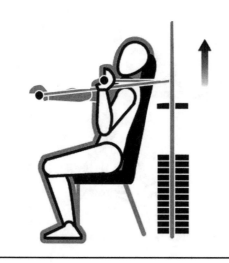

CHAPTER 4

Leg Exercises

In this section you will find exercises for all the muscles of the lower body. Most of the exercises listed work more than one set of muscles, but they have been grouped into the primary areas worked to make it easier to find the exercises. Try using a variety of exercises in your workouts to give you good overall leg development and strength.

10 SQUAT Place a bar in a squat rack and dip under the bar, positioning the bar across the shoulders about three inches below the vertebrae that protrudes at the base of the neck, with the load distributed across the back. Place your hands just outside your shoulders. Keep your head up, chest out, and shoulders back. Your back should be flat with a slight arch at the base; feet are shoulder width apart.

Take two short steps backwards out of the rack, keeping your feet shoulder width apart. Point your toes outwards at an angle of 30 to 35 degrees . Inhale deeply and contract the muscles of the torso to help

stabilize your upper body and keep your back flat. Descend by slowly lowering the buttocks towards the floor, keeping your hips under the bar as much as possible. Descend until the tops of the thighs are parallel to the floor. The ascent starts with a powerful drive to accelerate the weight out of the bottom position. Keep your head looking up to help counter forward lean. Keep the muscles of your torso contracted throughout the ascent phase of the lift. Continue to push with your legs until you come to a full standing position. Take another deep breath and descend for the next rep. Exhale as you pass through the sticking point near the end of the movement.

11 THE LEG EXTENSION Sit on a leg extension machine, adjusting the back support so that you are sitting up straight. Your leg should be bent to 90 degrees at the knee and aligned with the axis of rotation of the machine. The leg pad should be across your shin, just above your ankle. Straighten your leg until your lower leg is parallel to the floor, return the weight in a controlled manner to the starting position by bending at the knee. Do not jerk the weight out of the bottom position or bounce it at the top.

THIGH EXERCISES

12 FRONT SQUAT Place a bar in a squat rack. Grasp the bar with an overhand grip, hands just outside your shoulders, and rotate your elbows under the bar so that it sits across the front of the shoulders, tight against your throat. Keep your head up, chest out, and shoulders back. Your back should be flat with a slight arch at the base; feet are shoulder width apart.

THIGH EXERCISES

Take two short steps backwards out of the rack, keeping your feet shoulder width apart. Point your toes outwards at an angle of 30-degrees. Inhale deeply and contract the muscles of the torso to help stabilize your upper body and keep your back flat. Descend by slowly lowering the buttocks towards the floor, keeping your hips under the bar as much as possible. Descend until the tops of the thighs are parallel to the floor. The ascent starts with a powerful drive to accelerate the weight out of the bottom position. Keep your head looking up to help counter forward lean. Keep the muscles of your torso contracted throughout the ascent phase of the lift. Continue to push with your legs until you come to a full standing position. Exhale as you pass through the sticking point near the end of the movement. Take another deep breath and descend for the next rep. Your knees will travel forward over your toes more during the front squat than the squat, this keeps your torso upright so that you do not drop the bar.

13 **LEG PRESS** Sit in a leg press machine and place your feet on the push plate slightly wider than shoulder width apart. The feet should be placed high enough on the plate so that when the weight is lowered, the knees do not extend past the toes. Hands are on the mechanism that unlocks the push plate; head, shoulders and lower back remain in contact with the seat throughout the entire movement. Push up against the push plate and extend the legs until they are straight, but not locked. Move the handle so that the machine unlocks from the resting position. Lower the weight until there is a 90-degree angle between your hamstrings and calves, bringing your knees as close to your chest as possible. Straighten your legs and push the weight back up until your legs are

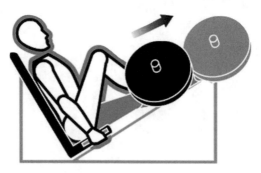

straight, but not locked. After the required repetitions are performed, extend the legs and move the locking mechanism back into place. After the locking mechanism is in place, slowly lower the weight until it is resting on the pins.

14 **SPLIT SQUATS** Hold a dumbbell in each hand or place a barbell across the back of the shoulders, and place your feet shoulder width apart. Keeping the torso upright, take a long step forward with one leg, allowing the front leg to bend to 90 degrees. . The back leg should be slightly bent. Keeping your torso upright at all times push off the heel of the front foot and straighten the front leg; then lower yourself back to the starting position. Do not step back to the upright position until you have done the required number of repetitions, then stand upright and switch legs, repeating the same number of repetitions.

HIP AND THIGH EXERCISES

15 **STEP UP** The box or bench used for this exercise needs to be high enough to create a 120-degree angle at the knee when the foot is placed on the box. Hold a dumbbell in each hand or place a barbell across the back of your shoulders as you would in the squat. Place your feet shoulder width apart; your head is up, your chest is out, and shoulders are back. Stand 12 to 18 inches behind the box or bench. Place the entire foot of one leg on the top of the box, shifting your weight to the leg on

the box. Powerfully extend the knee, hip, and ankle of the foot on the box, and bring your body to a standing position on top of the box. Step off the box, keeping all your weight on your working leg and lightly touch the ground with the non-working leg. Do not put any weight on the non-working leg—it is only being used as a guide to tell you when you have gone low enough. Immediately stand back up. Keep your trunk upright throughout the movement; avoid bending over from the waist.

HIP AND THIGH EXERCISES

16 **LATERAL STEP UP** The box or bench used for this exercise needs to be high enough to create a 120-degree angle at the knee when the foot is placed on the box. Hold a dumbbell in each hand or place a barbell across the back of your shoulders as you would in the squat; feet are hip width apart, head is up, your chest is out, and shoulders are back. Stand right beside the box or

bench. Place the entire foot of one leg on the top of the box, shifting your weight to the leg on the box. Powerfully extend the knee, hip, and ankle of the foot on the box, and bring your body to a standing position on top of the box. Step off the box, keeping all your weight on your working leg and lightly touch the ground with the non-working leg. Do not put any weight on the non-working leg; it is only being used as a guide to tell you when you have gone low enough. Immediately stand back up. When you have completed all the repetitions for one leg, move to the other side of the box and repeat the exercise for the other leg. Keep your trunk upright throughout the movement; avoid bending over from the waist.

HIP AND THIGH EXERCISES

17 **CROSSOVER STEP UP** The box or bench used for this exercise needs to be high enough to create a 120-degree angle at the knee when the foot is placed on the box. Hold a dumbbell in each hand or place a barbell across the back of your shoulders as you would in the squat; feet are hip width apart, head is up, your chest is out and

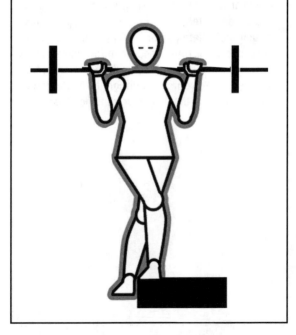

shoulders are back. Stand 12 to 18 inches to one side of the box or bench. Cross one leg in front of the other and place the entire foot of the leg that has crossed on the top of the box, shifting your weight to the leg on the box. Powerfully extend the knee, hip, and ankle of the foot on the box, and bring your body to a standing position on top of the box. Step off the box, keeping all your weight on your working leg and lightly touch the ground with the non-working leg. Do not put any weight on the non-working leg; it is only being used as a guide to tell you when you have gone low enough. Immediately stand back up. When you have completed all the repetitions for one leg move to the other side of the box and repeat the exercise for the other leg. Keep your trunk upright throughout the movement; avoid bending over from the waist.

HIP AND THIGH EXERCISES

18 LUNGES Place a bar in a squat rack and dip under the bar, positioning the bar across the shoulders at the top of the posterior deltoid with the load distributed across the back. Place your hands just outside your shoulders. Keep your head up, chest out, and shoulders back. Your back should be flat with a slight arch at the base; feet are shoulder width apart.

HIP AND THIGH EXERCISES

Take two long steps backward out of the rack and reset your feet so that they are shoulder width apart. Take a step forward with one leg landing heel first, shifting your weight from heel to toes. Continue to bend the lead leg until the top of your thigh is parallel to the ground. The back leg should bend until it is about one inch above the ground. Press the heel of the lead leg into the ground and push yourself back to an upright standing position. Repeat the same movement with the other leg leading.

HIP AND THIGH EXERCISES

19 **WALKING LUNGES** Walking lunges require enough space for you to take 6 to 8 long walking strides. Hold a dumbbell in each hand or place a barbell across the back of the shoulders; feet are shoulder width apart. Keeping the torso upright, take a long step forward with one leg, allowing the front leg to bend to 90 degrees. The back leg should be slightly bent. Shift your weight onto the front leg and stand back up, bringing the back leg forward. Step forward again, leading with the other leg. Continue this long striding motion for the prescribed number of repetitions.

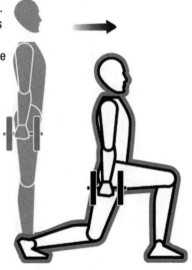

20 **LATERAL LUNGES** Place a bar in a squat rack and dip under the bar, positioning the bar across the shoulders at the top of the posterior deltoid with the load distributed across the back. Place your hands just outside your shoulders. Keep your head up, chest out, and shoulders back. Your back should be flat with a slight arch at the base; feet are shoulder width apart.

Take two long steps backward out of the rack and reset your feet so that they are shoulder width

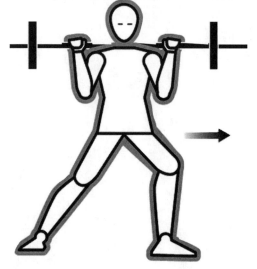

apart. Take a long step directly sideways with one leg, shifting your weight onto that leg and bending it until the top of your thigh is parallel to the ground. The other leg will be straight with the whole foot in contact with the ground. Press the lead foot into the ground and push your self back to an upright standing position. Repeat the same movement with the other leg leading. A set is completed once all the reps have been done on both legs.

HIP AND THIGH EXERCISES

21 CLOCK LUNGES Place a bar in a squat rack and dip under the bar, positioning the bar across the shoulders at the top of the posterior deltoid with the load distributed across the back. Place your hands just outside your shoulders. Keep your head up, chest out, and shoulders back. Your back should be flat with a slight arch at the base; feet are shoulder width apart.

Take two long steps backward out of the rack and reset your feet so that they are shoulder width

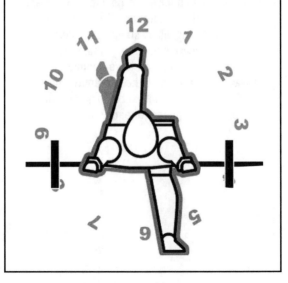

apart. Take a step straight forward with your right foot, where the 12 would be on a clock, landing heel first, shifting your weight from heel to toes. Continue to bend the right leg until the top of your thigh is parallel to the ground. The left leg should bend until it is about one inch above the ground. Press the heel of the right leg into the ground and push yourself back to an upright standing position. While continuing to face straight ahead, step forward and slightly to the right, placing your foot on the 1 of a clock face. Step back and repeat for 2, 3, 4, 5, and 6 o'clock all with the right foot. When stepping to 4 and 5 o'clock you will be stepping backwards and slightly sideways, so be careful about the balance in these steps. Once you have completed all the steps with the right foot, the left foot will do 12, 11, 10, 9, 8, 7, and 6 o'clock. A set is completed once all the reps are completed for each leg.

22 HIP EXTENSION

Facing a low pulley machine, attach the cable to your ankle. Stand upright with your feet shoulder width apart and hold onto the machine or some other support. The leg that is working should be extended in front of your body 10 to 12 inches. Keeping the torso upright, move the leg with the cable straight backwards as far as possible, pause, and return slowly to the starting position.

Do not bend forward from the waist in an attempt to increase the range of motion; maintain an upright torso at all times. This exercise can also be done with a piece of rubber tubing replacing the low pulley and cable.

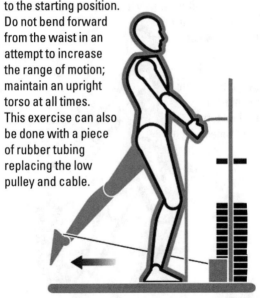

HIP AND THIGH EXERCISES

23 **HIP FLEXION** Stand facing away from a low pulley machine and attach the cable. Stand upright with your feet shoulder width apart and hold onto the machine or some other support. The leg that is working should be extended behind your body 10 to 12 inches. Keeping the torso upright bend the leg with the cable and raise your knee straight forward as far and as high as possible, pause, and return slowly to the starting position. Do not bend forward from the waist in an attempt to increase the range of motion; maintain an upright torso at all times.

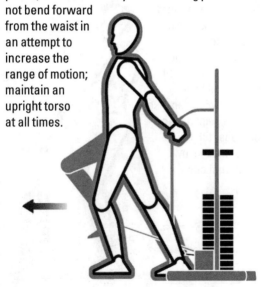

24 **HIP ADDUCTION** Facing sideways to a low pulley machine, attach the cable to the ankle closest to the machine. Stand upright with your feet shoulder width apart and hold onto the machine or some other support. The leg that is working is extended away from your body 18 to 24 inches. Keeping the torso upright, move the leg with the cable across your body as far as possible, pause, and return slowly to the starting position. Do not bend forward from the waist in an attempt to increase the range of motion; maintain an upright torso at all times. This exercise can also be done with a piece of rubber tubing replacing the low pulley and cable.

25 **HIP ABDUCTION** Facing a low pulley machine attach the cable to the ankle farthest from the machine. Stand upright, feet shoulder width apart, and hold onto the machine or some other support. The leg that is working should be crossed in front of your body 6 to 8 inches. Keeping the torso upright, move the leg with the cable straight sideways as far as possible, pause, and return slowly to the starting position. Do not bend forward from the waist in an attempt to increase the range of motion; maintain an upright torso at all times. This exercise can also be done with a piece of rubber tubing replacing the low pulley and cable.

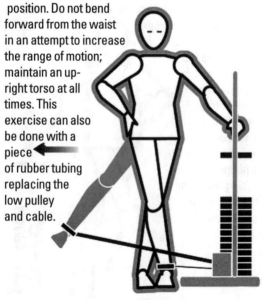

26 LYING LEG CURL Lie face down on the leg curl machine with your knees just off the end of the bench and your heels under heel pads. Hands should be holding onto the bench or handles on the machine. Keeping your upper body flat against the bench, curl your legs and raise the heel pads towards your buttocks. When the full range of movement has been completed, lower the weight to the starting position. Try to keep you hips on the bench at all times.

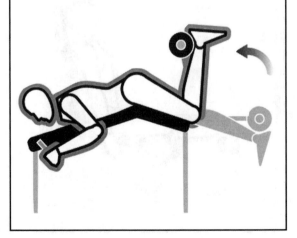

HAMSTRING EXERCISES

27 **SEATED LEG CURL** Sit on the seated leg curl machine, adjusting the back support so that you are sitting up straight, with your legs straight and knees just off the end of the bench, aligned with the axis of rotation of the machine. Your heels are on the heel pads. Bring the top support down so that it is tight against your thighs, preventing your legs from lifting off the bench. Bend your legs, pulling down on the heel pads until your legs are bent just past 90 degrees. Slowly allow your legs to straighten, returning to the starting position.

28 STANDING LEG CURL The standing leg curl is done one leg at a time. Stand facing the standing leg curl machine. Adjust the machine so that the thigh pad is placed just above your knee and your knee is aligned with the axis of rotation of the machine. The heel pad should be on your Achilles tendon, just above your ankle. Bend forward at the waist or hold on to the machine for support. Curl your leg and raise the heel pads towards your buttocks. When you have reached the top position, pause and slowly lower the weight back to the start. Do all repetitions with one leg before switching to the other.

29 **STANDING CALF RAISE** Use a calf raise machine, or place a bar across your back in a power rack. (This is a rack made up of two sets of vertical supports with adjustable parallel bars for safety.) Stand with the balls of your feet on a block 4 to 6 inches high, feet shoulder width apart. Lower your heels towards the floor as low as pos-

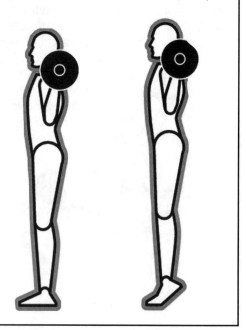

sible while keeping the balls of your feet on the block. Lift the weight by rising up on your toes as high as possible, pausing at the top for a second before lowering to the fully stretched position. Keep your legs straight but not locked throughout the movement. Make sure the movement is coming from the ankle and that you are not lifting the weight with the other leg muscles.

CALF EXERCISES

30 SINGLE LEG DUMBBELL CALF RAISE

Hold a dumbbell in one hand and stand with the ball of your foot on a block 4 to 6 inches high, bend the other leg behind the working leg. Lower your heels towards the floor as low as possible while keeping the ball of your foot on the block. Lift the weight by rising up on your toes as high as possible, pausing at the top for a second before lowering to the fully stretched position. Keep your legs straight, but not locked, throughout the movement. Make sure the movement is coming from the ankle and that you are not lifting the weight with the other leg muscles. You may hold onto a wall or other support for balance.

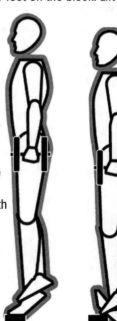

CALF EXERCISES

31 **CALF PRESS** Sit in a leg press machine and place the balls of your feet on the edge of the foot plate. Straighten your legs so that the weight is lifted 4 to 6 inches off the safety stops. Bending from only the ankle, lower the weight as low as possible and then press it back up, straightening your ankles and pushing with your toes. Hold the top position for a second and then lower to the fully stretched position again. This exercise can also be done with one leg at a time.

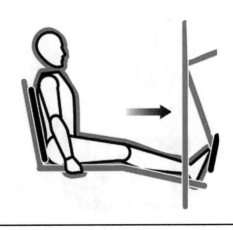

32 SEATED CALF RAISE

The seated calf raise works the soleus muscle, the muscle that lies under and below the gastrocnemius, the larger calf muscle. Sit on a seated calf raise machine with the balls of your feet on the foot supports and knees securely under the knee pads. Straighten your ankles and lift the weight off the safety stops, moving them out of the way with your hands. Bend at the ankles lowering your heels towards the floor. Lift the weight by rising up on your toes as high as possible, pausing at the top for a second before lowering to the fully stretched position again.

CHAPTER 5

Back Exercises

33 **THE DEADLIFT** Stand in front of a bar that has been placed on the ground, with feet shoulder width apart and the bar close to your shins. Squat down and grasp the bar with a mixed grip. Your feet are flat on the floor, hips are low, back is flat, head is up and shoulders are over the bar. Initiate the movement by pressing your legs into the floor lifting the weight. Keeping the weight close to your body continue to lift with your legs until the bar passes your kneecaps. Then bring your hips through and stand up straight. Incline your trunk forward slightly and bend your knees to lower the weight straight down to the floor. Keep your hips low, chest out, and shoulders back through-out the movement to keep your back flat and injury free.

34 **SUMO DEADLIFT** Stand in front of a bar that has been placed on the ground with feet 6 to 8 inches wider than shoulder width apart, toes pointed out at a 45-degree angle, and the bar close to your shins. Squat down and grasp the bar with a mixed grip. Your feet are flat on the floor, hips are low, back is flat, head is up and shoulders are over the bar. Initiate the movement by pressing your

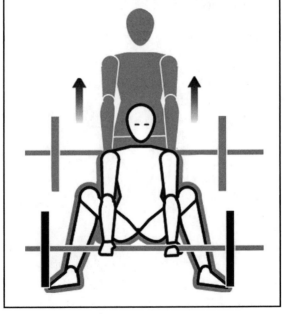

legs into the floor, lifting the weight. Keeping the weight close to your body, continue to lift with your legs until the bar passes your kneecaps. Then bring your hips through and stand up straight. Incline your trunk forward slightly and bend your knees to lower the weight straight down to the floor. Keep your hips low, chest out, and shoulders back throughout the movement to keep your back flat and injury free.

35 STRAIGHT LEG DEADLIFT

The bar starts on the floor, touching the shins. Feet are slightly wider than hip width apart. Bend at the waist, keeping the legs almost straight, with about 10 degrees of knee bend. Grasp the bar in with an overhand grip, placing the hands slightly wider than shoulder width apart. Your head is up, chest is out and shoulders are back. Your back is flat with a slight arch at the base. Keeping the bar as close to your body as possible, slowly pull the weight up, keeping your arms fully extended and your back flat. Think about keeping your trunk muscles tight and squeeze your buttocks as you straighten up. Slowly lower the bar back to the floor following the opposite path you used during the lift, reset your body and repeat for the required number of repetitions.

36 GOOD MORNINGS
Place a bar in a squat rack and dip under the bar, positioning the bar across the shoulders at the top of the posterior deltoid with the load distributed across the back. Place your hands just outside your shoulders. Keep your head up, chest out, and shoulders back. Your back should be flat with a slight arch at the base; feet are shoulder width apart. Take two short steps backwards out of the rack, keeping your feet shoul-

der width apart. Inhale deeply and contract the muscles of the torso to help stabilize your upper body and keep your back flat. Keep the knees bent slightly and bend forward from the hips, sticking your bottom out and moving your stomach towards your thighs. Your weight should be on the back half of your foot during the initial part of the descent. Continue to descend until your trunk is parallel to the floor or you feel your weight shift forward onto the balls of your feet. When you reach the bottom, pause and contract your glutes, hamstrings and lower back muscles to straighten your body up and return you to an upright position. Exhale as you pass through the sticking point near the end of the movement.

LOW BACK EXERCISES

37 **BACK EXTENSIONS** Lie face down on a flat bench or on a back extension bench with your waist just off the end of the bench. Your feet should be supported by the foot pads or a training partner. Cross your arms across your chest. Starting with your torso perpendicular to the floor raise your torso until it is parallel to the floor. Pause for a two count and slowly return to the bottom position. It is not necessary to raise your torso beyond parallel into a hyperextended position. As this exercise gets easier a weight can be held at your chest instead of crossing your arms.

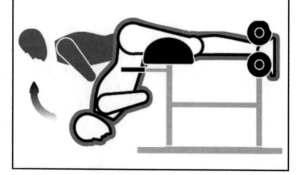

38 **REVERSE HYPERS** Lie face down on a high flat bench or on a reverse hyper bench with your waist just off the end of the bench. Your hands are holding onto the side of the bench or handles. Starting with your legs perpendicular to the floor raise your legs until they are parallel to the floor. Pause for a two count and slowly return to the bottom position. It is not necessary to raise your legs beyond parallel into a hyperextended position. As this exercise gets easier a weight can be held between your feet.

39 PULLDOWNS

PULLDOWNS Sit on the pulldown machine with knees under the leg supports. Take an overhand grip with hands slightly wider than shoulder width apart. Incline your trunk backwards about 10 degrees and pull the bar down in front of the body until it touches the top of the sternum. Slowly return the bar to the starting position. Keep the body still throughout the movement.

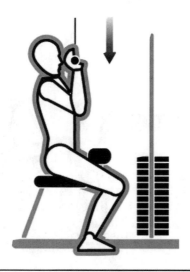

40 **SEATED ROW** Sit in front of a low pulley machine and grasp the handle with a narrow overhand grip. Your legs are slightly bent and your back is flat. Bending forward from the hips about 20 degrees, pull the handle towards your body initially by straightening the back. Once the handle reaches your knees, use the arm to finish the pull and bring the handle to the base of your sternum.

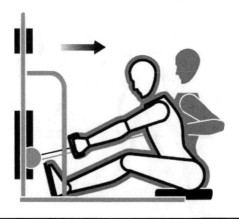

41 **ONE ARM DUMBBELL ROWS** Place one hand and knee on a bench. The opposite foot is firmly planted on the floor. Grasp a dumbbell in the hand not on the bench and, keeping the back flat throughout the movement, pull the dumbbell up until it touches your rib cage. Return the dumbbell to the start, allowing the arm to fully straighten so that you feel a stretch in the upper back and around the shoulder. Keep your shoulders parallel to the floor at all times; do not rotate your trunk to help lift the weight.

42 BENT OVER ROWS The bar starts on the floor, touching the shins. Feet are slightly wider than hip width apart. Bend at the waist, keeping the legs almost straight, with about 10 degrees of knee bend. Grasp the bar with an overhand grip, placing the hands slightly wider than shoulder width apart. Your head is up, chest is out and shoulders are back. Your back is flat with a slight arch at the base. Pull the bar up until it touches the base of the sternum, pause and slowly lower it back to the floor. Be sure to keep the back flat and abdominal muscles contracted throughout the movement.

43 **STRAIGHT ARM PULLDOWN** Stand or kneel in front of a pulldown machine so that the bar is just above eye level. Place both hands on the bar using an overhand grip, hands shoulder width apart. Keeping your body straight and upright, pull the bar down with straight arms until it reaches your waist and slowly return it to the start position.

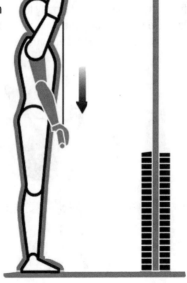

44 **PULLOVERS** Lie flat on your back on a bench, feet on the floor. Grasp a dumbbell in both hands with arms slightly bent. Beginning with the weight over the chest, lower the dumbbell back over the head keeping the elbows bent until the top of the dumbbell is even with the back of your head. Without bending the elbows any more, pull the bar back to the starting position.

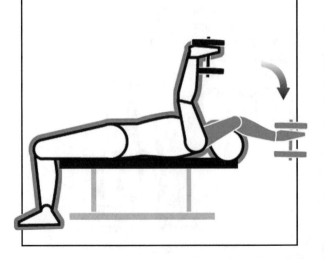

45 PULL UPS Reach overhead and grasp a pull up bar with an overhand grip, hands slightly wider than shoulder width apart. Lean back slightly from the waist to prevent hitting your head on the bar and flex the arms to pull your body up the bar. When your arms are fully flexed, the bar should be at the same height as your collarbone. Slowly straighten the arms until you have reached the starting position.

Shoulder Exercises

46 SEATED DUMBBELL OVERHEAD PRESS

Sit on a bench and grasp a dumbbell in each hand. Bring the dumbbells to the shoulders with hands facing forward. Keeping the muscles of the torso contracted to stabilize your upper body, push the weight overhead until the arms lockout. Lower the weight until the dumbbell touches the top of your shoulders.

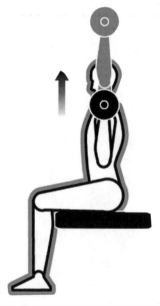

47 DUMBBELL OVERHEAD PRESS Standing upright, take a pair of dumbbells from the rack and bring them to your shoulders or have a training partner hand the dumbbells to you if they are too heavy for you to get to your shoulders on your own. Hands should face forward. Keeping the muscles of the torso contracted to stabilize your upper body, push the weight overhead until the arms lockout. Lower the weight until the dumbbell touches the top of your shoulders. Keep your trunk upright throughout the movement; do not lean backwards as you press the weight overhead.

48 OVERHEAD PRESS

Place a bar in a squat rack. Grasp the bar with an overhand grip, hands just outside your shoulders, and rotate your elbows under the bar so that it sits across the anterior deltoids, tight against your throat. Keep your head up, chest out, and shoulders back. Your back should be flat with a slight arch at the base; feet are shoulder width apart. Press the weight overhead until the arms are fully extended. Bend the elbows and control the weight back down to the shoulders and the starting position. As the weight approaches the shoulders, slightly bend the hips and knees to cushion the weight.

49 BENT LATERAL RAISES

Hold a dumbbell in each hand with palms facing each other. Sit on the end of a bench and bend at the waist so that your chest is on your thighs and the weight is just behind your calves. Keeping your elbows slightly bent, raise the weight to the side until your arms reach shoulder level and are parallel to the floor. Pause at the top of the movement and slowly lower the weight. Try to create a straight line across the shoulders from hand to hand; do not let the hands drift backwards as you raise the weight.

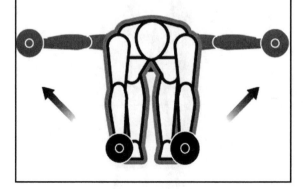

SHOULDER EXERCISES

50 **SIDE LATERAL RAISES** Standing up straight, hold a pair of dumbbells directly in front of you at waist height with palms facing each other. Keeping the elbows slightly bent, raise the weight directly to the side until the arms reach shoulder level and are parallel to the floor. Pause at the top of the movement and slowly lower the weight. Do not swing your body to help you lift the weight.

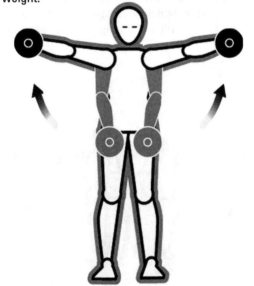

51 **FRONT RAISES** Standing up straight, hold a pair of dumbbells directly in front of you at waist height with palms facing your legs. Keeping the elbows slightly bent, raise the weight directly in front of you until your arms reach shoulder level and are parallel to the floor. Pause at the top of the movement and slowly lower the weight. Do not swing your body to help you lift the weight.

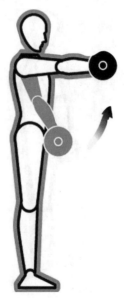

52 **REAR RAISE** Standing up straight, hold a dumbbell beside your leg at waist height with palms facing your leg. Keeping your elbow slightly bent, raise the weight directly backwards as high as you can without bending forward. Pause at the top of the movement and slowly lower the weight. Do not swing your body to help you lift the weight.

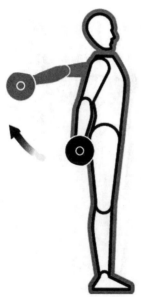

53 **45° RAISE** Standing up straight, hold a dumbbell beside your leg at waist height. The dumbbell should be positioned so that it is half way between a side lateral raise and a front raise. Rotate your hand so that your thumb is pointing towards your leg. Keeping your elbow slightly bent, raise the weight straight up from your thigh until your arm is at shoulder level and is parallel to the floor. Pause at the top of the movement and slowly lower the weight. Do not swing your body to help you lift the weight.

54 **LOW TRAP BALL EXERCISE** Lie face down on a stability ball so that your trunk is parallel to the floor, arms extended forward. Hold a light dumbbell in each hand with thumbs facing the ceiling. Starting with the dumbbells on the floor raise your arms until they are parallel to the floor. Hold for a second and lower them back to the floor. For variation try this with thumbs facing each other or facing the floor.

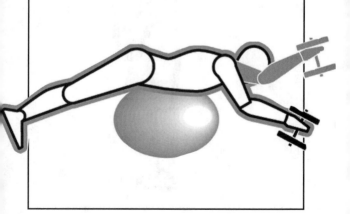

55 **TUBING EXTERNAL ROTATION** Attach a piece of rubber tubing to a doorknob or other apparatus so that it is just above waist height. Grasp the tubing in one hand so that it stretches across your body and has some tension. Bend your elbow to 90 degrees. Keeping your elbow close to your side, rotate your arm outwards, away from your body as far as possible.

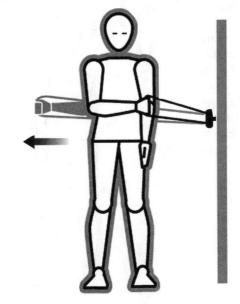

56 **90-90 EXTERNAL ROTATION** Stand with feet shoulder width apart, a dumbbell in one hand. Raise your arm so that your upper arm is parallel to the floor. Bend your elbow to 90 degrees so that your forearm is perpendicular to your upper arm with the palm of your hand facing forward. Keeping your upper arm parallel to the floor, rotate from your shoulder so that the dumbbell moves downwards towards the floor. Following the same arc used to lower, pull the weight back up to the starting position.

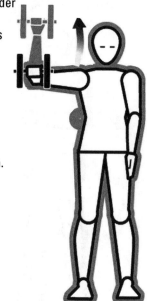

SHOULDER EXERCISES

57 **ALPHABET TRACING** Stand at arm's length from a wall, holding a basketball or medicine ball against the wall. Keeping your arm straight and body still, start outlining the letters of the alphabet with the basketball. Switch hands after you have completed all the letters.

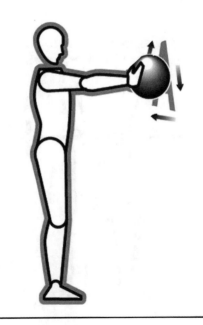

58 UPRIGHT ROW

Stand with feet shoulder width apart, hold a barbell in front of you with an overhand grip in the center of the bar, hands 6 to 8 inches apart. Keeping your upper body still, pull the weight up until it is level with the top of your sternum. Pause and lower it back to the starting position. Be sure to keep your elbows above the bar at all times.

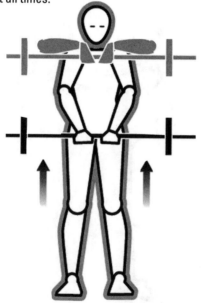

59 **BARBELL SHRUGS** Stand upright, feet shoulder width apart, knees slightly bent. Hold a barbell at arm's length in front of your body with an overhand grip. Slowly shrug your shoulders, raising them as high as possible. Pause for a moment at the top and lower the bar slowly, back to the starting position.

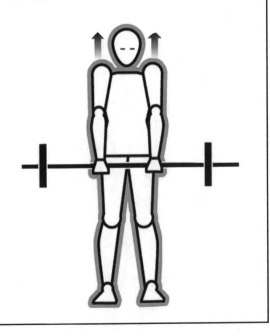

60 **DUMBBELL SHRUGS** Stand upright, feet shoulder width apart, knees slightly bent. Hold a dumbbell in each hand at arm's length, hands beside your body. Slowly shrug your shoulders, raising them as high as possible. Pause for a moment at the top and lower the bar slowly, back to the starting position.

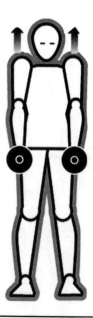

CHAPTER 7

Arm Exercises

61 BARBELL CURLS

Stand with feet shoulder width apart, knees slightly bent. Hold a barbell at arm's length in front of your body with an underhand grip, hands just outside your hips. Keeping your upper body still, bend at the elbow, flexing the arm and curling the barbell upwards until it is just under your chin. Slowly lower the weight, following the same arc used during the lift.

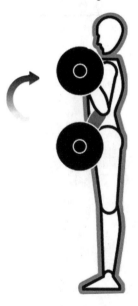

62 ALTERNATE DUMBBELL CURLS

Stand upright, feet shoulder width apart, knees slightly bent. Hold a dumbbell in each hand at arm's length, hands beside your body. Keeping your upper body still, curl one dumbbell up by flexing the elbow. As you start to lower the weight, begin curling the dumbbell in the opposite hand. Try to establish a rhythm of one weight going up while the other is being lowered.

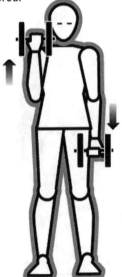

63 PREACHER CURLS

PREACHER CURLS Hold a barbell in both hands with an underhand grip, hands hip-width apart. Place your elbows over a preacher curl bench and lower the weight until your arms are straight. Bending from the elbows, curl the weight up as high as possible while keeping your elbows on the preacher curl bench. Pause at the top and slowly lower the weight until your arms are straight again.

64 CONCENTRATION CURLS

Sit on the end of a flat bench, feet spread apart. Hold a dumbbell in one hand with an underhand grip. Bend over slightly and place your elbow against the inside of your knee. Using your leg as a preacher bench, curl the dumbbell up as high as you can without lifting your elbow off your knee. Slowly lower the weight until your arm is straight.

65 **LYING TRICEPS EXTENSIONS** Lie flat on a bench, feet flat on the floor, hold a barbell with an overhand grip, your arms extended over your chest. Keeping your upper arms perpendicular to the floor, bend your elbows and lower the bar until it is just above your face. Keeping your elbows pointed towards the ceiling, straighten your arms and return the weight to arm's length. Your upper arms should stay still throughout the movement.

66 LYING DUMBBELL TRICEPS EXTENSIONS

Lie flat on a bench, feet flat on the floor, and hold a dumbbell in each hand, palms facing each other, your arms extended over your chest. Keeping your upper arms perpendicular to the floor, bend your elbows and lower the dumbbells until they are just above your face. Keeping your elbows pointed towards the ceiling, straighten your arms and return the weights to arm's length. Your upper arms should stay still throughout the movement.

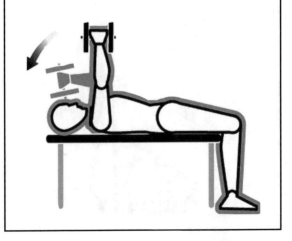

67 ONE ARM LYING DUMBBELL TRICEPS EXTENSIONS

Lie flat on a bench, feet flat on the floor, and hold a dumbbell in one hand with an overhand grip, your arm extended over your chest. The palm of your hand should be facing your feet. Keeping your upper arm perpendicular to the floor, bend your elbow and lower the dumbbell until it is just above your chest. Keeping your elbows pointed towards the ceiling, straighten your arms and return the weight to arm's length. Your upper arm should stay still throughout the movement.

68 TRICEPS KICKBACKS

Place one hand and knee on a bench. The opposite foot is firmly planted on the floor. Grasp a dumbbell in the hand not on the bench and, keeping the back flat throughout the movement, pull the dumbbell up until your upper arm is parallel to the floor and your elbow is tucked into your side and bent to 90 degrees. Keeping your upper arm parallel to the floor and your elbow tucked in to your side, straighten your arm so that your forearm is also parallel to the floor.

69 TRICEPS PUSHDOWN

Stand in front of a pulldown machine or other high pulley apparatus. Grasp a straight handle with an overhand grip, hands just outside your hips, arms straight, and the handle at waist height. Keeping your elbows tucked into your sides and upper arms still, bend your elbows, bringing your hands up as high as possible while still keeping your elbows tight against your sides. Push the weight back down following the same arc used during the lift.

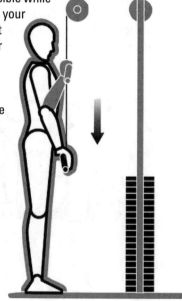

70 OVERHEAD TRICEPS EXTENSION

Stand upright with feet shoulder-width apart, knees slightly bent, holding a curl bar with an overhand grip, your arms extended over your head. Keeping your upper arms perpendicular to the floor, bend your elbows and lower the bar until it is just behind your head. Keeping your elbows pointed towards the ceiling, straighten your arms and return the weight to arms length. Your upper arms should stay still throughout the movement.

71 **WRIST CURLS** Sit on a bench with feet flat on the floor holding a barbell with an underhand grip, hands 8 to 12 inches apart. Bend over and place your forearms on the bench, your wrists just off the end of the bench and palms facing the ceiling. Extend your wrists and lower the weight as close to the floor as possible. Curl the bar as high as possible by flexing the wrists without raising the forearms.

palms up

72 REVERSE WRIST CURLS

Sit on a bench with feet flat on the floor holding a barbell with an overhand grip, hands 8 to 12 inches apart. Bend over and place your forearms on the bench, wrists just off the end of the bench, palms facing the floor. Bend your wrists and lower the weight as close to the floor as possible. Curl the bar as high as possible by extending the wrists without raising the forearms.

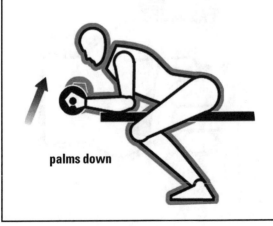

palms down

73 **HAND GRIPPER** Hold a hand gripper firmly in one hand. Squeeze the gripper until the ends of the handles touch. Slowly release the grip and repeat.

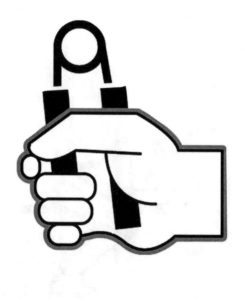

74 **PLATE PINCHING** Take a pair of weight plates—five or 10 lb plates will probably be sufficient to start. Place them together so that the plates are facing each other and the smooth side is facing out. Bend over and grasp the pair of plates between your fingers and thumb so that the plates are not in contact with the palm of your hand. Lift the plates off the floor 6 to 8 inches and hold them for as long as possible. Once you can hold the plates for 30 seconds either use heavier plates or sandwich a third plate between the first two.

75 **WRIST ROLLER** Stand with feet shoulder width apart and hold a wrist roller with weight attached at arm's length. Rotate the wrist roller and roll the cord up, raising the weight. Unroll the wrist roller and return the weight to the floor.

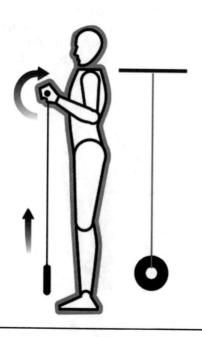

CHAPTER 8

Abdominal Exercises

76 **PARTIAL CURL UPS** Lie flat on the floor, knees bent to about 140 degrees, feet flat on the floor, hands on your thighs. Curl your trunk up and slide your hands along your thighs until they cover your knees. Slowly recline back to the start position.

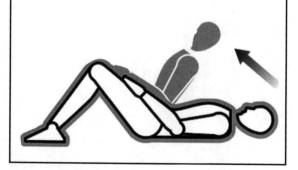

77 SIT UPS Lie face up on the floor, bend your knees to 90 degrees and keep your feet flat on the floor. Place your hands at your temples or fold them across your chest. Curl your torso up until your elbows touch the knees. Slowly uncurl until the shoulders touch the floor. A twisting motion that causes the opposing elbow and knee to touch can be done to involve the obliques. Perform the exercise smoothly, keeping the hips on the floor.

ABDOMINAL EXERCISES

78 **TRUNK ROTATION** Lie face up on the floor, bend your knees to 90 degrees and keep your feet flat on the floor. Arms are straight and extended towards the ceiling, holding a medicine ball. Sit up halfway into a sit-up position. Keeping your arms straight, rotate from the waist towards one side. Using the abdominal muscles only, pull the weight over and rotate to the other side. Perform the exercise smoothly; avoid quick jerky movements. Pull only with the abdominal muscles, not the arms.

ABDOMINAL EXERCISES

79 **LEG RAISES** Lie face up on the floor, legs straight, hands under your buttocks. Contract your abdominal muscles and force your lower back into the floor. Keeping your lower back tight against the floor, raise your legs until your feet are 4 to 6 inches above the floor. Hold for a second and slowly lower your legs to the starting position.

80 **HANGING LEG RAISES** Hang from a chin-up bar, palms facing forward, legs straight. Without swinging your body, slowly raise your legs until they are parallel to the floor. Slowly lower your legs to the starting position. This is an advanced exercise that should only be done after several months of the other abdominal exercises listed here.

81 **SIDE BENDS** Stand with your feet hip-width apart, holding a dumbbell in one hand at your side, palm facing your leg. Bend to the side, lowering the dumbbell down the side of your leg towards your knee. Straighten your trunk back up, continuing past the upright position, sliding your hand down your other leg towards your knee. After completing the required number of repetitions on one side, place the dumbbell in the other hand and repeat on the opposite side.

ABDOMINAL EXERCISES

82 **V-UP** Lie flat on your back, legs straight, hands extended overhead. Simultaneously bring your legs and trunk together, rising into a seated V position with legs in the air and trunk inclined. Hold this position for a two count and return to the ground, coming back up as soon as you touch the ground. Initially this drill will be done slowly until the balance point for your body is established. The drill should then become quicker and more explosive.

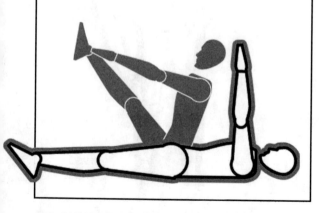

ABDOMINAL EXERCISES

83 **SIT UP TOSS** Lie on your back with knees bent and feet flat on the floor. Come to the top sit-up position and raise your hands overhead. Have a partner toss a medicine ball to your out-stretched hands, allowing the weight to take you back to the bottom of the sit up. As soon as your shoulder blades touch the ground explode upwards and toss the ball back to your partner. The power for the throw should be generated predominantly from the abdominal muscles with the arms only coming into play for the final toss.

84 **FRONT STABILIZERS** Lie flat on your stomach on the floor, legs straight. Rise up into a modified push-up position, bringing your arms under your shoulders so that your weight is resting on your forearms and toes. Keeping your abdominal muscles tight so that your back stays flat, hold this position for 15 to 30 seconds.

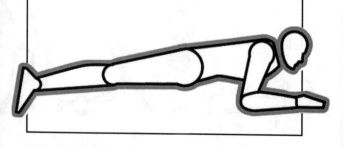

CHAPTER 9

Power Exercises

Power exercises can be done by anyone interested in adding some variety to their program but they are particularly effective for those who are training for a sport that involves running or jumping. Adding one or two power exercises to your sport-training program will improve your performance. Do not add too many power exercises, because they are very high intensity activities and can quickly lead to overtraining or injury if you do too much.

85 POWER SNATCH

To measure the optimal grip for the power snatch, extend one arm laterally so that it's parallel to the floor. Allow the other arm to hang down the side of the body. Measure the distance from the outside of the

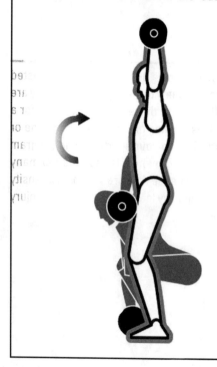

shoulder of the hanging arm to the knuckles of the closed fist of the other arm. This is the proper distance for placement of the index fingers while grasping the bar.

Position the bar at mid-thigh. Your head is up, chest out, shoulders are back and your back is flat with a slight arch at the base. Feet are hip-width apart, weight is on the front half of the foot. Hips are higher than the knees, shoulders are positioned over the bar. Arms are straight. Now rapidly extend the ankles, knees, and hips, in a jump-like motion. As your legs approach full extension, powerfully shrug your shoulders and pull your elbows up. Be sure to keep them in a position over the bar, allowing the bar to travel to sternum level. After the bar reaches sternum level and the body is fully extended, rapidly lower your body under the bar. Rotate the elbows forward and push up against the bar. Fully extend the arms so that the wrist, arm, and shoulder form a straight line.

86 POWER CLEAN

Grasp the bar with an overhand grip, hands slightly wider than hip-width apart. Position the bar at mid-thigh. Your head is up, chest out, shoulders are back and your back is flat with a slight arch at the base. Feet are hip-width apart, weight is on the front half of the foot. Hips are higher than the knees, shoulders are positioned over the bar. Arms are straight. Now rapidly extend the ankles, knees, and hips, in a jump-like motion. As your legs approach full extension, powerfully shrug your trapezius muscles and pull your elbows up. Be sure to keep them in a position over the bar, allowing the bar to travel to sternum level. After the bar reaches sternum level and your body is fully extended, rapidly lower your body under the bar. Rotate your elbows forward and under the bar, catching it on the anterior deltoids above your clavicles.

87 PUSH PRESS

The push press is similar to the overhead press with assistance from the legs to get the bar overhead. Place a bar in a squat rack. Grasp the bar with an overhand grip, hands just outside your shoulders and rotate your elbows under the bar so that it sits across the anterior deltoids, tight against your throat. Keep your head up, chest out, and shoulders back. Your back should be flat with a slight arch at the base; feet are shoulder width apart. Keeping the trunk muscles tight, dip down about four inches and explosively extend your legs and hips in a jump like motion, driving the weight overhead. As the weight passes your face press with the arms and push the weight to arm's length straight overhead. Lower the weight slowly, absorbing the weight with your legs as it returns to your shoulders.

88 MED BALL JUMP AND TOSS FOR HEIGHT

Stand with feet slightly wider than shoulder width apart, holding a medicine ball in both hands at waist height. Rapidly squat down to a quarter-squat position. Jump explosively upwards, driving with the legs and completely extending the trunk while accelerating the arms and ball upwards to toss the ball as high as possible. The majority of the power, and ball height, comes from the jump, which must be as high as possible.

89 TWO HAND TWIST TOSS

TWO HAND TWIST TOSS Stand sideways with the medicine ball in both hands at waist height. Twist downwards, pivoting on your feet and rotating at the trunk and hips. Quickly rotate in the opposite direction, driving through with your hips and coming onto your toes, in a movement similar to what you would use batting a baseball or hitting a golf ball. Keeping both arms straight, throw the ball as far as possible. The power for this throw comes from the pivot on the toes and firing of the hips around; it does not come from a rotation at the waist.

90 BOX JUMP

This drill requires a box or set of boxes, varying in height from 12 to 48 inches. The boxes should be solidly built with a non-slip landing surface. Stand facing the box with feet hip-width to shoulder-width apart, about an arm's length away from the box. Dip rapidly, swing the arms, driving them upwards, and jump onto the box. Jump just high enough to land on the box in a half-squat position. If you find you are pulling your knees up and landing in a deeper squat, the box is too high for this drill. Return to the ground by stepping down or hopping onto a soft mat.

91 STANDING VERTICAL JUMP This drill will help teach learning mechanics and serves as an introductory level exercise. Single vertical jumps can be used even if the athlete has not achieved the strength goals outlined in the chapter on getting started. Stand with feet about shoulder width apart. Swing the arms back and quickly dip until the knees bend to about 120 degrees. Explode upward, extending the knees, hips, ankles and trunk while swinging the arms forward and upward as explosively as possible. Focus on completely extending the body, reaching as high as possible. The arm drive is critical for achieving maximum jump height. This drill can be done under a basketball net or backboard so that athletes can monitor their progress and the consistency of their jumps.

92 TUCK JUMP This is an excellent drill for improving hip flexor strength and speed. The hip flexors are used extensively during sprinting activities. Assume the same starting position as in the vertical jump. Swing the arms back and jump as high as possible, extending the knees, hips, ankles and trunk. While in the air, quickly pull the knees into the chest, grabbing them with both hands prior to landing.

93 **ALTERNATE LEG PUSH OFF** Stand facing a solid box that can hold your body weight and place one foot completely on the box, the other foot remaining on the floor. When the foot is on the box the lower leg should be perpendicular to the floor and the thigh parallel to the floor creating a 90° angle at the knee. Swing both arms upward as explosively as possible and push off against the box, jumping as high as possible, completely extending your body, reaching upwards as high as possible. Switch feet in the air, landing with the opposite foot on the box. Immediately push off this foot and return to your original starting position.

CHAPTER 10

Balance and Stability Exercises

Balance and stability exercises are a good addition to a program for those who wish to add some variety to their exercises and challenge themselves. Most of these exercises can be done at home with equipment you can purchase from most fitness supply stores. Balance and stability exercises are lower intensity and are often used as part of a warm up before regular strengthening exercises with weights or machines.

FEET AND ANKLES

94 **SINGLE LEG BALANCE** This is a basic Balance Disc exercise. (The balance disk is an air filled disc that causes the foot to wobble, increasing the difficulty of balance exercises.) It allows the athlete to get used to the feel of the Balance Disc under the feet. Place one Balance Disc on the floor. Place one foot in the middle of the disc and raise the other foot to the front, 10 to 12 inches off the ground. Stand with shoulders back, chest out, upright posture, looking straight ahead. The difficulty of this drill can be increased by closing the eyes.

95 **POINTERS** Kneel down on all fours. Then place the Balance Disc under your right knee. Fully extend your right arm and left knee. Once the limbs are fully extended, place them back on the floor in the starting position.

96 MED BALL HIGH-LOW PASS

Stand across from a partner back to back; one or both can be standing on Balance Discs with one disc under each foot. Holding a medicine ball at arm's length, bend at the waist and pass the ball through your legs to your partner, keeping the legs as straight as possible. Your partner will then reach up and pass the ball back straight overhead. Try to establish a good rhythm and be sure to switch directions so that each partner has the opportunity to pass and receive between their legs.

97 SINGLE LEG TWIST AND REACH

Stand with one leg on a Balance Disc, a medicine ball on the ground at your side. Keeping the leg on the Balance Disc straight, twist to the side and bend over to pick up the medicine ball. Lift the ball diagonally so that it is raised over the opposite shoulder, at arm's length. Bend over, returning the ball to its original position on the floor and repeat, starting from a standing position each time.

98 **PARTNER MED BALL TOSS** Stand across from a partner. One or both can be standing on Balance Discs, one disc under each foot. Using a chest-pass motion, throw the ball back and forth. Be sure to stand far enough apart that you can throw the ball as hard as possible, which will allow you to develop both balance and power at the same time. This same drill can also be done with an overhead toss or standing on one leg.

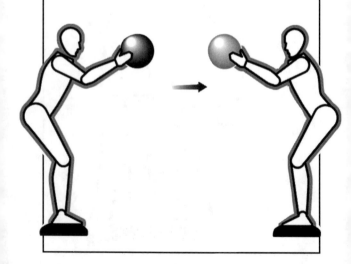

99 **ROMAN TWIST** Place a Balance Disc on the ground. Sit on the disc with your hands at the sides of your head, elbows out, and lean back slightly, feet flat on the floor, looking straight ahead. Rotate from the waist and turn slowly to one side as far as possible. Return to the center position and turn to the other side. Be sure to keep your feet flat on the floor.

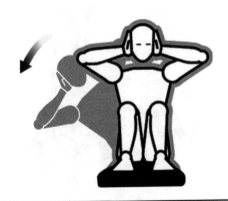

100 SINGLE LEG STABILITY BALL BALANCE

Choose a stability ball that will allow there to be a 90-degree angle at the knee when seated. Sit upright on the ball with shoulders back and chest out. Don't slouch. Keep your feet away from the ball and raise one leg so that it is parallel to the floor. Hold for 15 seconds, lower the leg and repeat with the other leg.

CHAPTER 11

Designing Your Program

Now that you have a repertoire of 100 exercises from which to choose, you need to start putting them into programs that will meet your training goals. While many people make changes to their program simply by changing to a different exercise, there are other factors—such as sets and reps, rest and recovery, and the speed with which you perform the exercise—that have an impact on your program. Learning to manipulate these variables will give you better results in less time and allow you to create an unlimited number of programs.

Sets and Reps

More than any other factor, the combination of sets and reps determines the outcome of the training program. The number of reps determines the weight that will be used, the lower the reps the heavier the weight. Generally, training with a heavy weight for fewer reps builds strength, an intermediate weight for a moderate number of reps will build muscle size and shape, and a light weight for many reps will build muscular endurance. The table below summarizes the combination of sets and reps for various training outcomes.

SETS AND REPS

GOAL	MUSCLE SIZE AND SHAPE	STRENGTH	MAXIMUM STRENGTH	MUSCULAR ENDURANCE
Sets per exercise	3-5	3-5	3-4	1 - 3
Repetitions	8-12	3-6	1-3	25-200
Sets per workout	12-30	10-32	5-20	8 - 1 0

SELECTING A WEIGHT TO USE

While the rep range gives you a guideline for the amount of weight to use, it is up to you to pick the appropriate resistance for your goal and fitness level. One of the most basic principals of training is the Overload Principal, which states that you need to continually be increasing the physical stress on your body in order for it to continue to adapt and bring you closer to your goals. Choose a weight that will allow you to just complete the number of reps required for the low end of the rep range, whether your goal is size and shape, strength, or endurance. Continue using this weight for your workouts, gradually increasing the number of reps performed until you are able to perform at the high end of the rep range for all sets. Then increase the weight so that again you can just finish at the low end of the rep range, and start over again.

TOTAL NUMBER OF SETS

It is not necessary to spend hours in the gym to get a good workout and achieve your goals. Many people try to do too much, believing that if one exercise is good, more must be better. This is untrue. The stimulus for increases in muscle strength or size is like the button on an elevator: press it and the elevator is coming; pressing the button more often does not get the elevator to your floor any faster. Doing more and more exercises and sets only increases the amount of time needed for recovery between training sessions, it does not provide a greater stimulus.

Initially one to two exercises per body part will be adequate, giving you a workout that should last no more than 40 minutes. As your fitness and recovery ability improves after three to four months of training, you can increase the number of sets to the range in the table above, giving you a workout that will take 60 to 90 minutes.

Rest between sets takes up the majority of the time in a workout. If you find that you cannot get a full workout done in the time you have available, you may want to consider either a split routine or circuit training.

Split Routines

Split routines are a way of organizing exercises so that you are working only a couple of body parts per training session. This decreases the time needed for each training session, but increases the number of times per week that you must work out. Typical groupings for a split routine are chest and triceps; back and biceps; legs and shoulders, with abs done every other workout. Another popular way of dividing things up is to simply split the body into upper and lower halves, working the upper body one day and the lower body the next, followed by a day off before starting the sequence again. Sample workouts in the next chapter for individual body parts will allow you to put together your own split routine program.

Circuit training

Circuit training as an alternative to the traditional set/rest style of training. Circuit training involves moving from one exercise to another, alternating upper and lower body movements, without any rest between exercises. After you have completed one set of the circuit, typically 4 to 8 exercises, you will take a break. The full body circuit in the next chapter can be done in less than 30 minutes if the gym is not busy.

Rest

Rest refers to the time that is taken between each set of an exercise. The rest between sets allows your body the time to replenish the energy used during the set and plays a role in determining the training effect. The amount of rest that is taken depends upon the duration of work in the strength training session and your training objectives.

STRENGTH

Rest periods for developing strength and maximal strength are quite long, usually 3 to 10 minutes. Strength training with heavy weight and low reps uses predominantly the anaerobic alactic energy system. The alactic energy system relies on the energy stored in the muscles. Energy is stored in the form of ATP and CP, two compounds, known as the phosphagens, which are available for immediate use. The stored supply of these compounds is relatively small, providing energy for about 10 to 15 seconds of all-out strength training effort. Once all the stored energy is used up, the body requires about three minutes to replace the phosphagens fully. If the next set is started before the phosphagens are fully restored, the muscles will be forced to use the anaerobic lactic energy system. This will result in a build up of lactic acid.

Lactic acid is responsible for the burning sensation in the muscles. It also causes feelings of heaviness and fatigue. A build up of lactic acid will inhibit the quantity and quality of work performed, resulting in fewer strength gains. If you feel these symptoms during your workouts it is a sign that you need to rest for longer periods.

MUSCLE SIZE AND SHAPE

It is quite common for bodybuilders to take short rest periods between sets, particularly during pre-contest preparation. This is done for a variety of reasons: depletion of carbohydrate stores, to keep metabolism high and burn more calories, and to stimulate muscle growth.

As we already discussed short rest periods will result in an accumulation of lactic acid. There is some evidence that strength-training sessions that result in high lactic acid levels also cause the body to naturally release more growth hormone, one of the hormones responsible for increasing muscle size. Rest periods in bodybuilding programs are typically 30 seconds to two minutes in duration.

SPORTS PERFORMANCE

The rest periods between sets for athletes will vary depending on the time of the year. They will initially be quite long, three to five minutes during the off season and preseason, when strength and power are the main training goals. During the season the rest period should simulate the rest periods that occur in their competitions. For instance, if you are a competitive weightlifter and have several minutes between lifts you should take several minutes between your sets. If you are a tennis player and have 20 seconds between points you should limit the rest time between your sets to about 20 seconds. A wrestler who is constantly working for a whole match may use circuit training in season so that he can continuously move from exercise to exercise. Adjusting the rest period between sets to your sport will help you develop the appropriate energy systems and recovery ability between bouts of work.

REST PERIODS BETWEEN SETS

WORK TYPE	REST BETWEEN SETS	REST BETWEEN EXERCISES
Strength	2-3 minutes	2-3 min
Maximum Strength	3-5 minutes	5-10 min
Muscle Size and Shape	30s-2 min	None
Sports Training	0-several minutes	0-several minutes

Recovery

Recovery, the time between training sessions, depends on your training goals and the number of sets and reps in a workout.

STRESS AND TRAINING ADAPTATIONS

The purpose of training is to create a stress and subsequent adaptation which results in an improved performance. Hans Selye was the first to popularize the concept of adaptations to stress in his book *The Stress of Life*. In this work, Selye proposes a three part response to stress called the General Adaptation Syndrome (GAS). The first stage, the alarm stage, is characterized by increases in stress hormones and activation of body defenses. The second stage, the stage of resistance, is a period where your body attempts to adapt so that homeostasis is restored. The third stage, the stage of exhaustion, occurs if the amount of stress is too great for your body to adapt. There is an increase in stress hormones and a reactivation of body defenses as in the alarm stage.

A training session imposes a stress on the body. Following the session there is a decrease in performance as a result of decreased energy stores or structural damage. At some point in time the body will replenish energy stores and repair damage. If enough time is left before the next training session, a training adaptation can occur and performance will be improved. If inadequate time is left and a training session is started before some level of adaptation occurs, your performance will continue to decrease.

The ideal time to start the next training session is when you reach the peak adaptation part of the curve; this is when your body has gotten as much as it can from the training session. The table below provides some guidelines for recovery periods based on training goals. The recovery number represents the minimum amount of time you should wait between training sessions, while the adaptation time is the point where your body is reaching peak adaptation from the previous training session. Note that this table refers to the time needed between training sessions for the same body parts. For instance, if you are following a split routine and are training to increase strength, you may be able to work out every day, but would only work each muscle group once every 96 hours.

GOALS	RECOVERY TIME	ADAPTATION TIME
Muscle size and shape	48 hours	72 hours
Strength	48 hours	96 hours
Maximum Strength	72 hours	120 hours
Muscular endurance	24 hours	72 hours

Exercise Speed

Strength increases are specific to the speed of movement at which the exercises are performed. If you train using slow movements you will increase your strength at low speeds, and if you train at high speeds you will get strong at high speeds. This makes speed of movement an important training variable that needs to be considered when designing a strength-training program. In real life you will encounter a variety of speeds of movement, from the slow, controlled movements you use when carrying something breakable to the violent high-speed movements you would use chopping wood or starting a lawn mower. Your strength-training program should reflect this by using a variety of speeds. Start with slow controlled movements for the first few weeks of your program and gradually increase the speed of movement as the weeks go on until you are performing the exercises in an explosive, dynamic fashion. Keep in mind that moving the weight fast is not a license to cheat or use bad exercise technique. High-speed movements must be done with perfect technique if you are to benefit from the exercise.

In the sample workouts in the next chapter the speed of movement is listed using three numbers; 111, 212, etc. These numbers are the three components of a lift; the concentric phase where the weight is lifted, a pause at the top or bottom of the movement, and the eccentric phase, where the weight is lowered. An exercise that is listed as a 111 will take you three seconds to complete each rep, and would be considered a moderate speed exercise. In some cases you will see Hold or Explosive. Hold is used for exercises that have little or no movement, requiring you to hold the position for a period of time rather than perform a number of reps. Explosive is used with the power exercises and indicates that the concentric portion of the exercise is to be done as fast as possible.

Order of Exercises

Placing your exercises in the proper sequence will ensure that you are getting the most benefit out of your workout. One of the goals of exercise sequencing is to arrange the exercises in an order that minimizes the impact of fatigue from exercise to exercise, allowing you to complete the workout before running out of energy. There are several ways of ordering your exercises depending on the equipment and time you have available and your training goals.

DESCENDING ENERGY COST ORDERING

Some ordering plans call for the sequencing of exercises from those that use the most energy to those that use the least. This allows you to train the hardest exercises without fatigue. Some examples of these schemes are the following:

Large Muscles to Small Muscles

Under this method the largest muscles of the body are trained before the smaller muscles. Training large muscles will require more energy and create more fatigue than training small muscles. The typical order would be:

Thighs and Butt	Abs
Hamstrings	Triceps
Chest	Biceps
Back	Calves
Shoulders	Forearms

Multi-joint to Single Joint

Multi-joint exercises are those where more than one major joint in the body is involved in the exercise. For instance in a deadlift, movement occurs at both the hip and knee joints. Movements involving multiple joints require heavier weights and more energy than single-joint movements. Examples of multiple-joint movements include:

Squats	Deadlift
Front squats	Overhead press movements
Bench Press	Bent rows
Incline press	Seated rows
Decline Press	

High Power to Low Power

Power is developed when the weight you are lifting is moved at high speed. This increases the energy demand of the activity. If speed of movement decreases, so does power production and the power training effect. The ability to maintain power depends on the body's stores of ATP, which are depleted very quickly. Power training is done early in the training session to take advantage of higher energy levels. The Olympic style weightlifting movements like the power clean, power snatch, push press, and jerk are the most common power movements.

ALTERNATING MUSCLE GROUPS

Alternating muscle groups is another way of preventing fatigue. The objective of this method is to alternate muscles from exercise to exercise. This is usually accomplished by alternating push and pull movements or upper body and lower body movements. For instance if you did an incline press as your first exercise you would want to do a seated row or pulldown as the next exercise because they use unrelated muscle groups. Alternating push pull exercises is used if you are only training a couple of muscle groups in each session. If you are doing a full-body workout, alternating upper and lower body is more effective. An example of ordering by alternating muscle groups is:

Push/Pull

Incline Bench Press
Seated row
Dumbbell Overhead press
Barbell Curl
Triceps Kickbacks

Upper Body/Lower Body

Bench press
Front Squat
Pulldown
Seated Leg curls
Side lateral raise
Standing Calf raise
Alternate Dumbbell curls
Sit ups
Triceps pushdowns

PRIORITY ORDERING

Priority ordering refers to sequencing the exercises by order of importance for your training goals. If you were training for rock climbing and need to increase the strength in your hands and fingers, you might choose to do forearm and gripping work first in a training session when you are fresh and have the most energy. This approach makes the most sense for activities that rely primarily on small muscle groups that typically fatigue quickly.

Warm Up

Warm up is an essential part of a workout. While originally thought to be primarily a means of preventing injury, it is now commonly accepted that the main purpose of warm up is to improve performance with injury prevention taking a secondary role. The positive effects of warm up occur because muscle temperature is increased, allowing the muscles to contract faster and more forcefully, use oxygen more efficiently, and eliminate waste better.

There are three types of warm ups: passive, general and specific. Each has its advantages and disadvantages.

PASSIVE WARM UP

A passive warm up increases temperature through external means. Massage, hot showers, lotions, and heating pads are common forms. Although these methods increase body temperature, they produce little positive effect on performance. A passive warm up, because of increased muscle temperature, may be suitable prior to a stretching exercise but should not be recommended as the sole means of warming up for intense physical activity.

GENERAL WARM UP

A general warm up increases temperature by using movements for the major muscle groups. Calisthenics and light jogging activities are the most common general warm ups. This type of warm up is meant to increase temperature in a variety of muscles using general movement patterns. This is a good warm up for a fitness class but should not serve as the sole form of warm up for athletic training or events.

SPECIFIC WARM UP

The specific warm up is designed to prepare you for the specific demands of the upcoming activity. The specific warm up helps psychological readiness, co-ordination of specific movement patterns, and prepares the central nervous system as well as the muscles. A specific warm up usually consists of a simulation of some technical component of the activity at work rates that increase progressively. For example, an Olympic weightlifter will perform the snatch with heavier weights progressively until reaching 80 to 90% of the opening attempt. Because of the rehearsal component of this type of warm up, it is the preferred method for high speed, strength and power activities.

Designing a warm up

A good warm up has both a general and specific component and may include a passive component if you feel you perform better when you use some sort of a topical analgesic like Tiger Balm.

GENERAL WARM UP

Full body Calisthenics

A warm up starts with some full body calisthenics. Exercises like jumping jacks, rope jumping, push ups, sit ups, and lunges are full body exercises that will increase body temperature. These exercises should be done for only 3 to 5 minutes at a time as the goal of warm up is to increase temperature, not create fatigue.

Stretching

Dynamic stretching is a more effective means of warm-up stretching than static stretching, meaning that rather than holding a stretch for a period of time you move through a full range of motion and then back to your starting position immediately without holding the stretch. This is particularly true when you are doing power training. Several studies have shown that a static stretch immediately before power training can significantly decrease subsequent power development.

Duration of General Warm Up

The amount of time needed to warm up depends on the type and intensity of the activity, as well as on environmental conditions. For someone engaged in a fitness workout program, 10 minutes should be sufficient for a warm up. Elite-level athletes may require 30 or 40 minutes to warm up, depending on the nature of their event, with higher-intensity events requiring longer warm ups. Exercising in a warm environment requires a shorter warm up than exercising in a cold one. In a normal environment, the onset of sweating is usually a good indicator that body temperature has increased sufficiently.

SPECIFIC WARM UP

The nature of the specific warm up depends on the activity that follows. Keep in mind that warm up is just that—warm up, not training. Fatigue should be kept to a minimum during warm up or the training session will suffer. When weight training, do at least two sets, one at 50% and one at 75% of the weight you will be using during the workout, before using the working weight. Very strong people need to do more sets. Many elite power-lifters and weightlifters use six to eight warm up sets prior to opening attempts in competition. Repetitions in warm up sets are low, 1 to 4, and done at a controlled speed. Warm up sets are done for every exercise in the program, not just the first exercise.

This chapter has provided you with a framework and background information to help you design your own training program. The following chapter provides a number of sample workouts that will help clarify these points. The workouts can be used as they are, or modified for your situation. If you do decide to create your own program, take your time and use a training log book to record the results of your efforts, this will help you refine your program as you progress.

Sample Workouts

The sample workouts in this chapter have been divided into upper body, which comprises the chest, shoulders, upper back, and arms; lower body made up of the legs, low back and abs; a full body program and power programs that can be used for sports training. Feel free to mix and match the different types of workouts to give you a program that best fits your schedule and goals.

The workouts can be used as they are or modified based on the guidelines in the previous chapter, increasing or decreasing the number of sets and reps to meet specific body shaping, strength or power training goals. If you find a program you like but do not have access to the equipment needed for a particular exercise, refer back to the appropriate exercise chapter and choose a substitute that works the same body part.

Upper Body Workouts

DUMBBELL WORKOUT

This workout is done using only dumbbells and a bench, making it a convenient home or on-the-road workout.

EXERCISE	SETS	REPS	SPEED
Dumbbell Bench Press	3	8	111
One Arm Dumbbell Row	3	8	111
Side Lateral Raise	3	8	111
Bent Lateral Raise	3	8	111
Dumbbell Arm Curls	3	8	111
Dumbbell Triceps Extension	3	8	111

BALANCED WORKOUT

This workout uses a mix of machines and free weights to increase strength and muscular fitness in all the muscles of the upper body.

EXERCISE	SETS	REPS	SPEED
Tubing External Rotation	3	8	111
Incline Press	3	8	111

Seated Row	3	8		111
Overhead Press	3	8		111
Side Lateral Raise	3	8		111
Concentration Curls	3	8		111
Kickbacks	3	8		111
Wrist Curls	3	8		111

STRENGTH PROGRAM 1

This program is designed to build strength in the upper body muscles. Over a three-week period you will gradually increase the weight you are using and decrease the number of reps. At the end of the three weeks, decrease the weight a bit and increase the reps back to the week 1 reps.

EXERCISE	SETS	REPS (one week each box)			SPEED
Bench Press	4	8	6	4	111
Flys	4	8	6	4	111
Bent Row	4	8	6	4	111
Pulldowns	4	8	6	4	111

EXERCISE	SETS	REPS			SPEED
Overhead Press	4	8	6	4	111
Bent Lateral Raise	4	8	6	4	111
Barbell Curls	4	8	6	4	111
Triceps Extension	4	8	6	4	111

STRENGTH PROGRAM 2

This program is a continuation of Strength Program 1 and should be used after 2 to 3 cycles of Strength Program 1. It is very high intensity and not meant for beginners. This program will peak your strength level. Do only one cycle of this program before switching back to something less intense. Rest periods between sets need to be quite long, 3 to 5 minutes, and the program should be done twice a week at most.

EXERCISE	SETS	REPS (one week each box)			SPEED
Dumbbell Bench Press	4	6	4	3	111
Dips	4	6	4	3	111
Straight Arm Pulldowns	4	6	4	3	111
Pull Ups	4	6	4	3	111
Dumbbell Overhead Press	4	6	4	3	111

5 X 5

The 5 x 5 program is a classic program used by power-lifters when training for competition. It provides the optimal combination of sets and reps to build both muscle mass and strength. The 5 x 5 program should be used only 1 to 2 times per week. If you choose to do the program once a week, which is highly recommended the first time you try it, you should do the strength maintenance program on the other upper-body training day. All reps are done as explosively as possible. The weight may not move very fast because it is heavy; it is the intent to move as fast as possible that is most important.

EXERCISE	SETS	REPS	SPEED
Bench Press	5	5	Explosive
Overhead Press	5	5	Explosive
Overhead Triceps Extension	5	5	Explosive
Shrugs	5	5	Explosive
Bent Row	5	5	Explosive
Alternate Dumbbell Curls	5	5	Explosive

Strength Maintenance Program

This program can be used as a light day when doing one of the strength programs or the 5 x 5 program. It is also a great program for athletes who need to maintain their strength during the competitive season or those who have reached their goals and just want to maintain their present fitness and strength level.

EXERCISE	SETS	REPS	SPEED
90-90 External Rotation	3	6	212
Dumbbell Incline Press	3	6	212
One Arm Dumbbell Row	3	6	212
Pullovers	3	6	212
Triceps Pushdowns	3	6	212
Barbell Curls	3	6	212

Individual Body Part Programs

Individual body part programs are done as part of a split routine, which has been discussed on page xxx. The repetitions listed in the program are for a mixed program that will improve strength and cause a small amount of muscle mass increase, ideal for those seeking a "toned" physique. If you wish to focus primarily on strength, decrease the reps into the 3 to 5 reps range. If you wish to maximize muscle mass increase the reps into the 10-12 range and add an additional set to each exercise. Rest periods between sets will be quite long, 2 to 4 minutes.

ARM PROGRAM

EXERCISE	SETS	REPS	SPEED
Alternate Dumbbell Curls	3	6	112
Preacher Curls	3	6	112
Lying Triceps Extensions	3	6	112
Kick Backs	3	6	112
Triceps Pushdown	2	6	112

CHEST PROGRAM

EXERCISE	SETS	REPS	SPEED
Bench Press	3	6	112
Decline Press	3	6	112
Cable Crossovers	3	6	112
Flys	3	6	112

UPPER BACK PROGRAM

EXERCISE	SETS	REPS	SPEED
Pulldowns	3	6	112
Straight Arm Pulldown	3	6	112
Seated Row	3	6	112
Low Trap Ball Exercise	3	6	112

SHOULDER PROGRAM

EXERCISE	SETS	REPS	SPEED
Tubing External Rotation	3	6	112
90-90 External Rotation	3	6	112
Upright Row	3	6	112
Side Lateral Raise	3	6	112
Front Raise	3	6	112
Bent Lateral Raise	3	6	112

FOREARM AND GRIP PROGRAM

EXERCISE	SETS	REPS	SPEED
Hand Gripper	4	6	112
Wrist Roller	4	6	112
Plate Pinching	4	20 seconds	112
Reverse Wrist Curl	3	6	112

Lower Body Workouts

DUMBBELL WORKOUT

This workout is done using only dumbbells and a bench, making it a convenient at home or on the road workout.

EXERCISE	SETS	REPS	SPEED
Step Ups	4	8	111
Walking Lunges	4	8	111
Standing Calf Raise	4	8	111
Straight Leg Deadlift with Dumbbells	4	8	111

BALANCED WORKOUT

This workout uses a mix of machines and free weights to increase strength and muscular fitness in all the muscles of the lower body.

EXERCISE	SETS	REPS	SPEED
Squat	3	8	111
Lateral Step Up	3	8	111
Lying Leg Curl	3	8	111
Standing Calf Raise	3	8	111
Hip Adduction	3	8	111
Hip Abduction	3	8	111

STRENGTH PROGRAM 1

This program is designed to build strength in the upper body muscles. Over a three week period you will gradually increase the weight you are using and decrease the number of reps. At the end of the three weeks decrease the weight a bit and increase the reps back to the week 1 reps.

EXERCISE	SETS	REPS (one week each box)			SPEED
Squats	4	8	6	4	111

EXERCISE	SETS	REPS (one week each box)			SPEED
Straight Leg Deadlift	4	8	6	4	111
Leg Press	4	8	6	4	111
Lying Leg Curl	4	8	6	4	111
Standing Calf Raise	4	8	6	4	111

STRENGTH PROGRAM 2

This program is a continuation of Strength Program 1 and should be used after 2 to 3 cycles of Strength Program 1. It is very high intensity and not meant for beginners. This program will peak your strength level. Do only one cycle of this program before switching back to something less intense. Rest periods between sets need to be quite long, 3 to 5 minutes, and the program should be done twice a week at most.

EXERCISE	SETS	REPS (one week each box)			SPEED
Front Squat	4	6	4	3	111
Lying Leg Curl	4	6	4	3	111
Split Squats	4	6	4	3	111
Good Mornings	4	6	4	3	111
Calf Press	4	6	4	3	111

5 X 5

The 5 x 5 program is a classic program used by power-lifters when training for competition. It provides the optimal combination of sets and reps to build both muscle mass and strength. The 5 x 5 program should be used only 1 to 2 times per week. If you choose to do the program once a week, which is highly recommended the first time you try it, you should do the strength maintenance program on the other upper-body training day. All reps are done as explosively as possible. The weight may not move very fast because it is heavy; it is the intent to move as fast as possible that is most important.

EXERCISE	SETS	REPS	SPEED
Squats	5	5	Explosive
Reverse Hypers	5	5	Explosive
Seated Leg Curl	5	5	Explosive
Standing Calf Raise	5	5	Explosive

STRENGTH MAINTENANCE PROGRAM

This program can be used as a light day when doing one of the strength programs or the 5 x 5 program. It is also a great program for athletes who need to maintain their strength during the competitive season or those who have reached their goals and just want to maintain their present fitness and strength level.

EXERCISE	SETS	REPS	SPEED
Leg Press	3	6	212
Lying Leg Curls	3	6	212
Clock Lunges	3	6	212
Single Leg Dumbbell Calf Raise	3	6	212
Leg Extensions	3	6	212

LEG PROGRAM

EXERCISE	SETS	REPS	SPEED
Squats	3	6	112
Crossover Step Ups	3	6	112
Hip Abduction	3	6	112
Hip Adduction	3	6	112
Seated Leg Curls	3	6	112
Seated Calf Raise	3	6	112

LOW BACK PROGRAM

EXERCISE	SETS	REPS	SPEED
Good Mornings	3	6	112
Reverse Hypers	3	6	112
Back Extensions	3	6	112

ABDOMINAL PROGRAM

EXERCISE	SETS	REPS	SPEED
Partial Curl Up	3	15	112
Side Bends	3	12	112
Leg Raises	3	15	112
Front Stabilizers	3	20 seconds	Hold

Power Workouts

POWER WORKOUT 1-CONTACT SPORTS

This program is designed to build power for sports such as basketball, hockey, and football. Over a three-week period you will gradually increase the weight you are using and decrease the number of reps. At the end of the three weeks decrease the weight a bit and increase the reps back to the week 1 reps.

EXERCISE	SETS	REPS (one week each box)			SPEED
Power Clean	4	8	6	4	111
Box Jump	4	8	6	4	111
Front Squats	4	8	6	4	111
Straight Leg Deadlift	4	8	6	4	111
Bench Press	4	8	6	4	111
Seated Overhead Press	4	8	6	4	111
Bent Row	4	8	6	4	111
Sit Ups	4	8	6	4	111

POWER WORKOUT 2 –NON-CONTACT SPORTS

This program is designed to build strength for racquet sports and sports like volleyball, baseball, softball and soccer. Over a three-week period you will gradually increase the weight you are using and decrease the number of reps. At the end of the three weeks decrease the weight a bit and increase the reps back to the week 1 reps.

EXERCISE	SETS	REPS (one week each box)			SPEED
Med Ball Jump and Toss for Height	4	8	8	8	Explosive

Standing Vertical jump	4	8	8	8	Explosive
Alternate Leg Push Off	4	8	6	4	Explosive
Squats	4	8	6	4	111
Leg Curl	4	8	6	4	111
90-90 External Rotation	4	8	6	4	111
Incline Press	4	8	6	4	111
Pulldowns	4	8	6	4	111

POWER WORKOUT 3- JUMPS AND THROWS

This program is designed to build power using minimal equipment through jumps and throws. Over a three-week period you will gradually increase the height you are jumping and decrease the number of reps. At the end of the three weeks decrease the height a bit and increase the reps back to the week 1 reps.

EXERCISE	SETS	REPS (one week each box)			SPEED
Box Jump	3	12	10	8	Explosive
Tuck Jump	3	12	10	8	Explosive
Med Ball Jump and Toss for Height	4	12	10	8	Explosive

Two Hand Twist Toss	4	12	10	8	Explosive

POWER WORKOUT 4- OLYMPIC-STYLE LIFTS

This program is designed to build power using primarily the Olympic-style lifts. Over a three-week period you will gradually increase the weight you are using and decrease the number of reps. At the end of the three weeks decrease the weight a bit and increase the reps back to the week 1 reps.

EXERCISE	SETS	REPS (one week each box)			SPEED
Power Snatch	3	5	4	3	Explosive
Power Clean	3	5	4	3	Explosive
Push Press	3	5	4	3	Explosive
Squats	3	5	4	3	111
Incline Press	3	5	4	3	111
Bent Row	3	5	4	3	111

POWER CIRCUIT

This full-body power circuit can be completed in about 20 minutes if the gym is not too busy. Move as quickly as possible from exercise to exercise, taking a rest only after you have completed the whole circuit. When you can do the prescribed number of reps in the prescribed time-increase the weight you are using. Try to be as explosive as possible for the concentric portion of all exercises.

EXERCISE	CIRCUIT I S TIME/REP	CIRCUIT II TIME/REP	CIRCUIT III TIME/REP	CIRCUIT IV TIME/REP	CIRCUIT V TIME/REP
Squat	10s/4	10s/4	10s/4	10s/4	10s/4
Bench Press	10s/4	10s/4	10s/4	10s/4	10s/4
Leg Curl	10s/4	10s/4	10s/4	10s/4	10s/4
Pulldown	10s/4	10s/4	10s/4	10s/4	10s/4
Calf Press	15s/10	15s/10	15s/10	0	0
Overhead Dumbbell Press	10s/4	10s/4	10s/4	10s/4	10s/4
Back Extension	15s/ 6	15s/ 6	15s/ 6	15s/ 6	15s/6
Leg Raises	15s/ 6	15s/ 6	15s/ 6	15s/ 6	15s/ 6
	Rest 2 min	Rest 2 min	Rest 2 min	Rest 2 min	

Full body Workouts

DUMBBELL WORKOUT

This workout is done using only dumbbells and a bench making it a convenient at-home or on-the-road workout.

EXERCISE	SETS	REPS	SPEED
Step Ups	2	8	111
Lunges	2	8	111
Dumbbell Bench Press	2	8	111
Side Lateral Raise	2	8	111
Bent Lateral Raise	2	8	111
One Arm Dumbbell Rows	2	8	111
Pullovers	2	8	111
Concentration Curls	2	8	111
One Arm Lying Dumbbell Triceps Extensions	2	8	111
Single Leg Dumbbell Calf Raise	2	8	111
Side Bends	2	8	111
C url Ups	2	8	111

BALANCED WORKOUT

This workout uses a mix of machines and free weights to increase strength and muscular fitness in all the muscles of the body.

EXERCISE	SETS	REPS	SPEED
Front Squat	3	8	111
Standing Leg Curl	3	8	111
Standing Calf Raise	3	8	111
Incline Dumbbell Bench Press	3	8	111

STRENGTH PROGRAM 1

This program is designed to build strength in all muscles. Over a three-week period you will gradually increase the weight you are using and decrease the number of reps. At the end of the three weeks decrease the weight a bit and increase the reps back to the week 1 reps.

EXERCISE	SETS	REPS (one week each box)			SPEED
Leg Press	4	8	6	4	111
Incline Bench Press	4	8	6	4	111
Pulldowns	4	8	6	4	111
Back Extension	4	8	6	4	111

EXERCISE	SETS	REPS (one week each box)			SPEED
Side Lateral Raise	4	8	6	4	111
Low Trap Ball Exercise	4	8	6	4	111
Alternate Dumbbell Curls	4	8	6	4	111
Triceps Kickbacks	4	8	6	4	111

STRENGTH PROGRAM 2

This program is a continuation of Strength Program 1 and should be used after 2 to 3 cycles of Strength Program 1. It is very high intensity and not meant for beginners. This program will peak your strength level. Do only one cycle of this program before switching back to something less intense. Rest periods between sets need to be quite long, 3 to 5 minutes, and the program should be done twice a week at most.

EXERCISE	SETS	REPS (one week each box)			SPEED
Sumo Deadlift	4	6	4	3	111
Dips	4	6	4	3	111
Dumbbell Overhead Press	4	6	4	3	111
One Arm Dumbbell Row	4	6	4	3	111
Bent Lateral Raise	4	6	4	3	111
Barbell Curls	4	6	4	3	111
Triceps Pushdowns	4	6	4	3	111

20-MINUTE CIRCUIT

This full body circuit can be completed in about 20 minutes if the gym is not too busy. Move as quickly as possible from exercise to exercise, taking a rest only after you have completed the whole circuit. When you can do the prescribed number of reps in the prescribed time, increase the weight you are using.

EXERCISE	CIRCUIT I S TIME/REP	CIRCUIT II TIME/REP	CIRCUIT III TIME/REP	CIRCUIT IV TIME/REP	CIRCUIT V TIME/REP	TOTALS
Seated Row	15s/ 8	15s/ 8	15s/ 8	15s/ 8	Rest 15s/	32 reps
Leg Press	15s/ 6	15s/ 6	15s/ 6	15s/ 6	15s/ 6	30 reps
Bench Press	15s/ 6	15s/ 6	15s/ 6	15s/ 6	15s/6	30 reps
Leg Curl	15s/ 6	15s/ 6	15s/ 6	15s/ 6	15s/6	30 reps
Arm Curl	15 s/10	15 s/10	15 s/10	15s/0	Rest 15s/	30 reps
Calf Raise	15s/15	15s/15	15s/0	15s/0	Rest 15s/	30 reps
Overhead Press	15s/ 6	15s/ 6	15s/ 6	15s/ 6	15s/6	30 reps
Back Extension	15s/ 6	15s/ 6	15s/ 6	15s/ 6	15s/ 6	30 reps
Triceps Pushdown	15s/ 10	15s/ 10	15s/ 10	15s/0	Rest 15s/	30 reps
	Rest 2 min	Rest 2 min	Rest 2 min	Rest 2 min		

INDEX